Francis William Newman

Reminiscences

Of two exiles (Kossuth and Pulszky) and two wars (Crimean and Franco-Austrian)

Francis William Newman

Reminiscences
Of two exiles (Kossuth and Pulszky) and two wars (Crimean and Franco-Austrian)

ISBN/EAN: 9783337012571

Printed in Europe, USA, Canada, Australia, Japan

Cover: Foto ©ninafisch / pixelio.de

More available books at **www.hansebooks.com**

REMINISCENCES

OF

TWO EXILES

(KOSSUTH AND PULSZKY)

AND

TWO WARS

(CRIMEAN AND FRANCO-AUSTRIAN)

BY

F. W. NEWMAN, M.R.A.S.

EMERITUS PROFESSOR OF UNIVERSITY COLLEGE, LONDON
ONCE FELLOW OF BALLIOL COLLEGE, OXFORD
NOW HONORARY FELLOW OF WORCESTER COLLEGE, OXFORD

LONDON
KEGAN PAUL, TRENCH & CO., 1, PATERNOSTER SQUARE
1888

REMINISCENCES,
ETC.

ANY one who reads the title of this work may naturally ask, What peculiar knowledge of such topics can this author have had? and, What connection with Hungary had these two wars? To both questions the following pages will give reply; but I at once state, as a general augury of my knowing something, that when the two Hungarian celebrities, Kossuth and Pulszky, quitted England in 1860, Pulszky told me they were glad to leave behind in ME one Englishman who knew all their secrets and could be trusted to expound them.

At that time I knew what part Kossuth had taken in encouraging the Turks to accept the war forced on them by the Czar Nicolas; but near a quarter of a century had to pass before her Majesty Queen Victoria revealed to us the signal impetus given to the Western Powers against Russia, of which to this day the Right Honourable John Bright seems ignorant. I find middle-aged men hardly to know who and what Kossuth was, and to have no other notion of the Crimean war than that which the Quakers have diligently inculcated for thirty years.

No one for a moment denies that the war was dreadful, and I knew, before Mr. Gladstone told us in 1880, that the Aberdeen ministry were intensely reluctant to enter it; but that it has been useless, I cannot agree. To Germany, Austria, Hungary, and Italy, it has been eminently beneficial; but Kossuth truly said we brought it on ourselves, by unrighteously evading our duty of mediating for Hungary. If England and France had not fought it, nothing short of an equivalent war must have been fought against Russia by other powers. The instinct of England and of the Prince Consort urged it, not unwisely, as I judge, but upon an unwilling ministry.

I must make myself somewhat prominent in telling reminiscences. That my relations with Kossuth were cordial may be inferred even from the fact, that I earned his thanks by collecting the newspaper reports of his American speeches, and digesting them into a readable book. With his political ally, Pulszky, I keep up to this day friendship and occasional correspondence. Not that I was ever so serviceable to Kossuth as one Englishman of rare attainments, the late Joshua Toulmin Smith, a constitutional lawyer, well versed in old English institutions and a zealot for Hungary. While Kossuth was still in harbour at Southampton, Toulmin Smith boarded his ship, and to his astonishment handed to him a precise manuscript that gave details concerning the local history and affairs of Southampton. Not many hours later, the great Hungarian, responding in English to his warm reception by the mayor and other authorities, seemed to have a truly marvellous acquaintance with our English municipalities. A like service, on several other occasions, the same gentleman, quite unsolicited, performed; nor could his valuable aid be rejected. Great as Kossuth was in himself, he became to us wonderful by the varied extent of his knowledge and the command which he had of it all. No such claim of introduction to him had I; no such knowledge of Hungarian institutions as Toulmin Smith; but first Pulszky, whose acquaintance I formed in the Hungarian Committee, found it worth while to impart to me minute details of the Austro-Hungarian quarrel, and Kossuth, on his arrival afterwards, quickly learned that he could trust me. Indeed, when the English Bluebook on Hungary was published (as usual, too late to avert calamity), I learned to the bottom how righteous was the Hungarian cause.

The rich men of the city of London, of Birmingham, of Manchester, and other towns in Scotland and England, mourned over Hungary and honoured Kossuth (its ex-governor) as representing the brave and just nation whose liberties, as ancient as those of England, were crushed by the conspiracy of two emperors. The mass of our intelligent artizans were still more eager in the same cause. I cannot be far wrong in saying that one hundred and thirty-seven municipalities entreated Kossuth to address them; but at the end of 1851 he hurried to America, invited by the President of the United States to traverse the Union as "the guest of the Republic." He already foresaw (what *our* statesmen either did not see, or thought it wiser *not* to see) that the Emperor Nicolas would not let slip his opportunity of attacking Turkey, while Austria was his humble servant and Hungary in feud with her; while also Austria would gladly accept from him Turkish Bosnia or Wallachia as a sop. Kossuth, certain that Austria in the next move of Nicolas would play his game, expected the Sultan to rouse Hungary against Austria, and was anxious to press on America for a recognition of Hungarian belligerence, *if* Hungary again became belligerent; and further, if possible to induce the president to ask of the sultan welcome for an American squadron on a convenient Greek island (say, Mityléné), to facilitate diplomatic relations. Thus minded, Kossuth left England while zeal for Hungary was at white heat. He returned after a few months, and nearly all that zeal seemed to have evaporated—why, may presently be explained. Our newspapers have had plenty of new topics to dwell on, and in the thirty-six years which have since past (1888) have never had reason to recur to that history. In consequence few indeed in England now know why England was so deeply moved.

I therefore here insert a paper issued in November, 1849, by the London Hungarian Committee, in which I took an active part.

"1. Hungary is an ancient Constitutional Monarchy, which used to *elect* its kings. Every new king was solemnly crowned with the crown of St. Stephen, after taking the coronation oath on Hungarian soil, and signing the solemn personal engagement. In the year 1687 the royalty was made *hereditary* in the family of Hapsburg; but, so far was Hungary from becoming a province of Austria, to this year not a single Austrian has been allowed to hold office in the Hungarian kingdom. An Austrian is *a foreigner* in Hungarian law and practice.

"2. The kings of the House of Hapsburg have, notwithstanding, made various attempts to overthrow the liberties of Hungary. After repeated attempts to fuse Hungary into Austria, and repeated insurrections, a long struggle begun by Leopold I. was ended in 1711 by Joseph I., who was constrained * to confirm the old Constitution. Again, by the efforts of Joseph II. to enforce the German language, and suppress the municipalities, a revolt was kindled, which his successor Leopold II. finally pacified (in 1790) only by withdrawing all his brother's innovations, and by making a peculiarly distinct avowal, that (Art. 10) '*Hungary with her appanages is a free kingdom, and in regard to her whole legal form*

---

* The peace of Szatmar was pressed on Austria by "the Maritime Powers," *England* and Holland.

of government (including all the tribunals), independent; that is, entangled with no other (non obnoxia) *kingdom or people, but having her own peculiar consistence and constitution; accordingly to be governed by her legitimately crowned king after her peculiar laws and customs.'* Nevertheless, Francis I. dared to violate his coronation oath by not assembling the Diet from 1811 to 1825. At last he was compelled to give way by the passive resistance to all government.* From that year onward the Hungarians have struggled successfully for internal reforms by constitutional methods, though perpetually thwarted by the bigotry, ignorance, and perverse ambition of the Austrian Cabinet or Crown.

" 3. The internal reforms which they desired were chiefly the following :—To remove or lessen the distinctions between the privileged and unprivileged classes; and improve the principles of taxation and of the tenure of land. Next, to extend perfect toleration of religious creed to all. The high Magyar nobility are

* See note A, p. 24.

generally Roman Catholics; yet they have been as willing to concede toleration as the lower nobility and middle classes, who are generally Protestants. Thirdly, to establish Free Trade with all nations. For the Austrian Cabinet chose to confine this great country to Austria for its market, while treating Hungarian produce as foreign. Fourthly, to maintain a free press, and the right especially of publishing the debates and proceedings of the Diet. Fifthly, in general, to develop the great resources of Hungary by all sorts of material improvement in agriculture, in roads, in bridges. To this of late has been added a struggle for general education.

"4. One mode of resistance applied by Austria was to extinguish Parliamentary Bills by the *veto* of the Crown, the fear of which paralyzed the Upper House—a body always naturally disposed to lean to Austria. Against this, the Hungarians had no adequate constitutional weapon to use, since the Austrian Cabinet was not responsible to the Hungarian Diet. The often-repeated legal declaration of their independence, and in particular the distinct compact of Leopold II. in 1790-91, justified them in desiring, by peaceful and constitutional means, to attain an independent ministry directly responsible to their own Parliament.

"5. Such a ministry had been long talked of and claimed in the Diet. In fact, the Conservative party and the Opposition had differed little as to the *objects* at which they aimed, but chiefly as to the *vehemence* with which they should press them; the Conservatives pleading to "give time" to the Austrian Cabinet. But in March, 1848, the Conservatives, as a separate party, vanished, by the great mass of them acceding to the Opposition. Kossuth carried a unanimous vote, that the Constitution of Hungary could never be free from the eternal machinations of the Austrian Cabinet, until Constitutional Government was established in the foreign possessions of the Crown, so as to restore the legal *status* of the period at which the Diet freely conferred the royalty on the

House of Hapsburg. This vote paralyzed the Austrian authorities. Vienna rose against Matternich, and a revolution took place there. A constitution and a National Guard were enacted. The Hungarian Diet immediately claimed for itself also a responsible ministry. This was granted without delay, and Count Louis Batthyanyi was made Premier. But *on the very same day*, March 15, Jellachich was appointed Ban [Duke] of Croatia. In a letter to Vienna, dated March 24, 1848, the Archduke Stephen, Viceroy of Hungary, is found to have suggested three modes of destroying the Hungarian Constitution: *either* to excite the peasants against the nobles, as in Gallicia, and stand by while the parties slaughter each other; or to tamper with Batthyanyi's honesty; or to invade and overpower Hungary by military force. A transcript of this letter in the archduke's handwriting was afterwards found among his papers, when he fled from Pesth, and was officially published with all the necessary verifications. The Austrians have not dared to disown it.

"Before March ended, a deputation of all the leading members of both Houses from Hungary appeared in Vienna, carrying to the king their unanimous claim that he would consent to various Bills. In these the greatest constitutional change was, the restoration of the old union between the Diets of Hungary and of Transylvania. But socially, the most important laws were, the equalizing of all classes and creeds, and the noble enactment which converted the peasants into freeholders of the soil, quit of all the old feudal burdens. This Bill had passed both the Houses by February 4, 1848, *before the French Revolution had broken out;* so little had that great event to do with the reforming efforts of the Hungarians. The Austrian Cabinet, seeing their overwhelming unanimity, felt that resistance was impossible. Accordingly, Ferdinand proceeded with the Court to Pressburg, and ratified the laws by oath. This is the Reform of April 11, 1848, which all patriotic Hungarians fondly looked upon as their charter of constitutional rights, opening to them the promise of a career in which they should emulate Great Britain, as a pattern of a united, legal, tolerant, free, and royal country.

"6. Croatia is a province of the Hungarian Crown; and there Jellachich, as governor, openly organized revolt against Hungary, by military terrorism and by promising Slavonic supremacy. On Batthyanyi's urgency, King Ferdinand *declared Jellachich a rebel*, and exhorted the Diet to raise an army against him; but always avoided finally to sanction their Bills. Meanwhile Radetzky [in Italy] defeated Charles Albert [of Savoy]. Jellachich dropped the mask of Croatianism, and announced to Batthyanyi that there should be no peace until a ministry at Vienna ruled over Hungary. In September, as the king [an imbecile] would neither allow troops to be raised in Hungary, nor the Hungarian regiments to be recalled from Italy for home-defence, a Hungarian deputation was sent to the Austrian Diet; but it was denied admittance by aid of the Slavonic party. To catch stray votes (it seems), Latour,

Austrian minister at war, in the Diet, September 2, solemnly disavowed any connection with Jellachich's movement ; yet on September 4 a Royal ordinance (officially published in Croatia only), *reinstated Jellachich in all his dignities;* who, soon after, crossed the Drave to invade Hungary with a well-appointed army 65,000 strong. As he openly showed the king's commission, Batthyanyi resigned, September 9, since he did not know how to act *by* the king's command *against* the king's command. No successor was appointed, and the Hungarian Diet had no choice but to form a Committee of Safety. To embarrass them in this, the king reopened negotiations with Batthyanyi, September 14, but still eluded any practical result by refusing to put down Jellachich. Meanwhile, September 16, despatches were intercepted, in which Jellachich thanked Latour for supplies of money and material of war. The Hungarian Diet published them officially and distributed them by thousands. But Hungary was still unarmed, and Jellachich was burning, plundering, slaughtering.

September 25, Lamberg was sent to Pesth, in the illegal character of Imperial Commissary of Hungary; but was immediately murdered by the rage of the populace. Masses of volunteers were assembled by the eloquence of Kossuth, which, with the aid of only 3000 regular troops, met and repulsed Jellachich at Sukoró, September 29, and chased him out of their country. But Latour was far too deep in guilt to recede. A Royal rescript of October 3 dissolved the Hungarian Diet, forbade all municipal action, superseded the judicial tribunals, declared Hungary under martial law, *and appointed Jellachich civil and military governor of that country, with discretionary power of life and death,* and an expressly unlimited despotism. It likewise distinctly announced the determination of the Crown* to incorporate Hungary into Austria. Troops from Vienna were publicly ordered by Latour (October 6) to march against the Hungarians. This order, coupled with alarm inspired

* I seem to remember that its first words were, "Hungary exists no longer."

by the approach of Jellachich (whose defeat was kept secret) led to the *émeute* in Vienna, in which Latour was murdered—a murder which was made a pretext for bombarding Vienna, and destroying the newly sanctioned Constitution. Windischgrätz, the agent in this work, joined his forces to those of Auersperg, who meanwhile had sheltered Jellachich.

"At all this the Hungarians were so infuriated, that, after deposing the generals (who were believed traitorously to have allowed Jellachich to escape), with inferior artillery, and with forces not half of the Austrians, who were 75,000 strong besides their reserves, they fought and lost the battle of Schwechat, October 30. This was the *first* and *last* battle fought by the Hungarians on Austrian soil—fought only against those who were protecting a ruthless enemy, who had desolated Hungary by countless outrages: yet this is trumpeted by the Austrians as Hungarian aggression. Jellachich (November 2) entered Vienna in triumph, and was entrusted with a great army in the course of the whole war that followed. It is then impossible to doubt that the Austrians had supplied him with arms, money, and authority from the beginning, and that *they* began this bloody war by combined violence and treachery, while Hungary was in profound peace.

"7. The Cabinet now tried to obtain from Ferdinand a direct permission to carry into detail the rescript of October 3, and seize Hungary by right of conquest. But as Ferdinand began to be troubled with religious scruples, they resolved to depose him, and put his nephew on the throne—a youth of eighteen, educated by the Jesuits, and accustomed to obey his mother the Archduchess Sophia, who was so identified by the Viennese with the Cabinet as to be called the Lady Camarilla.

"By intrigue of some sort, they induced the half-witted emperor to sign the act for his own abdication [if indeed he ever signed it], and at once seated Francis Joseph in his place; who, not having taken the coronation oath, might be assured by his directors that he committed no wrong in invading the laws and constitution of Hungary! An Austrian army marched into the country, and in the course of January and February overran and occupied it as far as the Theiss eastward, and as high as the Marosch northward; the Russians meanwhile penetrated into Transylvania. The usurpation of the archduchess and Cabinet seemed to have triumphed.

"8. On March 4, 1849, Count Stadion published his new Constitution for fusing down Hungary into a part of the Austrian Empire. If previously Hungary had been under Russian despotism, this Constitution would have seemed highly liberal; and, from an Austrian point of view, such it was; but to the Hungarians it was an intolerable slavery. First, it virtually annihilated their municipalities, and subjected their police to Vienna. Next, it would have enabled the Austrian Cabinet to put in Austrian civil and military officers everywhere in Hungary— an innovation as odious to the Hungarians, as would *French* police magistrates, excisemen, overseers, colonels, and lord-lieutenants be to the *English* nation. Thirdly, it swamped their Parliament among a host of foreigners, ignorant of Hungary and its wants, and incapable of legislating well for it. Fourthly, it was enacted, without the pretence of law, by the mere stroke of Count Stadion's pen. If the Hungarian Constitution, fourteen times solemnly sworn to by kings of the House of Hapsburg, was to be thus violated, what possible security could the nation have for this new-fangled Constitution of Stadion, if it were ever so good in itself? If they admitted such a right in the Austrian Crown, in six months a new ordinance might reduce them under a pure despotism. In the face of wrong so intense, it is not worth while to name secondary grievances; but it was most bitterly felt, that *such* was the reward of the constant loyalty of Hungary to the House of Hapsburg, and *such* the sequel of that solemn act by which Ferdinand had so happily ratified their recent glorious reforms!

"On reviewing the Constitutional question, it

was clear to the Hungarians, *first*, that Ferdinand had no legal power to abdicate without leave of the Diet, which leave it was impossible to grant, since in the course of nature Ferdinand might yet have direct heirs ; *secondly*, that if he became incapacitated, it was the right of the Diet to appoint a Regent ; *thirdly*, that if Ferdinand had died, Francis Joseph was not the heir to the Hungarian Crown, but his father, Ferdinand's brother : *fourthly*, that allegiance is not fully due to the true heir, until he has been crowned ; *fifthly*, that if Francis Joseph had been ever so much the true heir and had been ever so lawfully crowned, the ordinances would be a breach of his oath, essentially null and void, and equivalent to a renunciation of his compact with the people ; *sixthly*, that even to Austria the Ministry of Stadion,—or rather of the archduchess,—was no better than a knot of intriguers, which had practised on the clouded intellect of the sovereign to grasp a despotism for itself ; while over Hungary it had no more ostensible right than had that of Prussia or

France. All Hungary therefore rose to resist, Slovachs and Magyars, Germans and Wallachs, Catholics and Protestants, Gipsies and Jews, nobles, traders, and peasants, rich and poor, Progressionists and Conservatives. Ferdinand was still regarded as their legitimate, but unlawfully deposed, king.

"9. Between the Theiss and the Marosch, Kossuth had organized the means of fabricating arms and money; and in the course of March and April a series of tremendous battles took place, in which the Austrians were some fifteen times defeated, and without a single change of fortune their armies, 130,000 strong, were swept out of Hungary with immense loss. Only certain fortresses remained in their power, and those were sure to fall by mere lapse of time. The Austrian Cabinet was desperate at losing a game on which it had risked so much. Its more scrupulous members had retired, including Stadion himself. Bloodier generals were brought forward, and the intervention of Russia (long promised, and granted as early as February in Transylvania) was publicly avowed. This act finally alienated from Austria every patriotic Hungarian.

" 10. Upon the entrance of the Russians with the consent of Francis Joseph, the Hungarian Parliament, on the 14th of April, after reciting the acts of perfidy and atrocity by which the House of Hapsburg had destroyed its compacts with the nation, solemnly pronounced that House to have for ever forfeited the crown. During the existing crisis, Kossuth, according to constitutional precedent, was made governor of the country. * * * * * *

" 12. The *English Crown* is peculiarly affected by these events [the overthrow of Hungarian law], because they destroy the confidence of nations in the oaths of princes; especially considering that Hungary was the only great community on the continent, whose ancient liberties had not been violently and treacherously annihilated by its king. No guarantees of right any longer exist, except those which have been wrested out by popular violence, and established on some *doctrinaire* basis. The *Aristocracy* of England are deeply concerned, when the only remaining continental aristocracy possessed of constitutional rights and taking the lead of a willing nation, is remorselessly trampled under foot. Our *Commonalty* is concerned, when deprived of commercial intercourse with fourteen millions of agriculturists. Our *religious* feelings are shocked, when Hungarian zeal for universal toleration is overridden by the Romanist bigotry of Austria. Our *liberties* are endangered by the spectacle of two sovereigns tearing in pieces a noble nation from pure hatred of its constitutionalism, which nine centuries have not made sacred in their eyes. The security of *all Europe* is endangered, by the virtual vassalage of Austria to Russia, which this calamitous outrage has entailed; for Austria is now so abhorred in Hungary, that she cannot keep her conquest except by Russian aid. Every one foresaw this from the beginning : the Government of Vienna knew it, as well as that of St. Petersburg. Such are the results of the conspiracy of an Austrian Cabinet against their emperor, against his kingdom of Hungary, against the new-born liberties of Vienna, and against the balance of power in Europe."

NOTE A.

[It may be worth while to explain how, in 1825, the Austrian Emperor Francis was affrighted into juster dealing.

The brothers of Alexander I. of Russia were Constantine and Nicolas. Constantine, elder of the two, was an active soldier, untempered, violent, and wayward; often cruel, always severe, and greatly hated as Governor of Russian Poland. The Imperial House looked forward with alarm to his possible succession to the Crown; but a wayward nature is sometimes wayward in love, and such was Constantine. Though married to an amiable Coburg princess, he desired to divorce her, in order to marry a beautiful Polish lady; but without Alexander's active aid, the legal difficulties could not be removed. Alexander assented, on the condition that Constantine should sign abdication to the Crown. No one then can have expected Alexander to die childless, and Constantine is believed to have accepted the condition. On the sudden death of Alexander by fever from long travel, Constantine displayed dutiful loyalty to his brother Nicolas, his junior by seventeen years; but when his abdication was proclaimed at St. Petersburg, he was at Warsaw, and the army at St. Petersburg did not believe it. A Republican conspiracy of the officers impelled them to declare Constantine emperor, and Nicolas had to meet a short but alarming civil war. The tidings of this much alarmed Francis in Vienna, and showed him that reconciliation with Hungary was his only safe course. Thus Hungary regained her Parliament in 1825.]

Kossuth, in accepting the post of Governor, had insisted that in the future settlement Europe would have a voice, and royalty was only in *suspense.* He believed that no patriotic Hungarian remained an advocate of royalty longer than he did; and if it had been possible, he would have joyfully welcomed a son of Queen Victoria as King of Hungary.

Quaker zeal has recently reasserted that Lord Palmerston was the great effector of the Crimean war. This urges me to narrate, that after many public meetings in the autumn of 1853, urging Parliament to assist the sultan in the war which the Czar Nicolas had forced upon him, Lord Dudley Stuart impressed me to accompany him in a deputation to Lord Palmerston, who was then Home Secretary. My friend Pulszky soon after remarked to me that Lord Dudley Stuart was too simple-hearted a man to deal with the adroit Palmerston, who, as Foreign Secretary, had always amused him and made him a tool; but Lord Dudley was sure of a kind reception from Palmerston, and brought with him some zealous Marylebone tradesmen. Palmerston listened very graciously to all the speeches; but, in reply, represented the great military power of Russia and the immense uncertainty of a war against her on land ; so far indeed was he from encouraging us to hope for aid to the sultan, that he let nothing escape from him to imply that he himself was in favour of it. I suppose this may have been in November.

My Hungarian friends could not explain Lord Palmerston's conduct as Foreign Secretary. Not contented with repulsing Kossuth's envoy in 1848 by a simple historical falsehood, saying that England knew nothing of Hungary but as a province of the Austrian Empire ; he even instantly notified to Vienna that he had given this repulse, as if to signalize his zeal for Austria. After Russia's intended intervention was notorious, the war became European, and was not confined to Austria and Hungary. Palmerston must have known of the treaty of Szatmar, which England, aided by Holland, almost forced upon Austria for her own purposes. Our Blue-book on Hungary showed how faithfully the noble lord had been informed that

Austria had outrageously broken that treaty. In our Parliamentary debate of 1849 Palmerston had cast censure and scornful pity on Austria, but had skilfully evaded the real question, the intervention of Russia. Elsewhere he called "a strong Austria a European necessity," but he knew that to be at feud with Hungary, her greatest kingdom, made Austria weak, not strong. Mere prudence counselled early mediation, lest Russia get advantage. Some secret power seemed to paralyze him. Had Palmerston even published the Blue-book early enough, it might have been of great avail. Not only was mediation refused, but belligerency was not acknowledged, not even when Hungary was victorious; and it might even be suspected that the sultan was deceived by the ambassadors into the unlawfulness of selling arms (according to European law) to a victorious nation whose belligerency was a broad fact, however other nations might choose to shut their eyes to it. When England was eminent in establishing the peace of Szatmar, she was bound to take notice of its gross and wicked violation. Did some one *behind* Palmerston forbid him? So it seemed. As if in mockery, on August 1, 1849, after the treason of Görgey, a Hungarian general, had ruined Hungary, Lord Palmerston offered to mediate, *if Austria desired it!* He earned by it only bitter insult from the Austrian Premier, Schwarzenburg.

I suppose that Kossuth and Pulszky were as ignorant as was I of the agency and post of Stockmâr, a physician ennobled as Baron, whom the first King of Belgium gave to Prince Albert as a foreign counsellor. When this baron died, his son published a biography of him, which first revealed to us his existence and his potency. Evidently our ministers could not afford to thwart him, nor were allowed to take measures lest he read their secret despatches. A new thought instantly arises, when we learn that a private Belgian was retained by the Queen's Royal Consort to advise him on foreign policy. Lord John Russell, as Premier, was forced to dismiss Lord Palmerston from the

Foreign Office, for the offence of sending off a despatch before the queen had seen it. The belief was, that the noble lord did not wish the despatch to leak out, through the prince, to foreigners who had no right to see it. In how galling a curb the prince kept our Foreign Secretary the queen has been pleased to publish for our information, when she allowed Sir Theodore Martin to draw for us a picture of the noble lord agitated to tears by the reproaches of the prince. It is now open to believe that Stockmâr and his Austrian policy (indeed, the King of Belgium wanted an Austrian princess as his son's wife) sometimes drove Palmerston to despair, and our diplomacy into heartlessness.

That Belgian policy was bitterly hostile to Hungary, was soon after coarsely proved. The Austrians rudely and cruelly prosecuted Kossuth's two sisters for treason; but failing to prove anything against them, exiled them. These two, with a third sister and his mother, somehow found their way to Belgium; that an Austrian officer *deposited* them there, I find hard to believe. The mother, aged and declining, longed to see her son once more; but the Belgian Government in 1852 refused permission to Kossuth to come from England to see her, unless he would consent to be accompanied everywhere by a policeman. The mother indignantly spurned such a condition, and forbade his coming. What had loyal Belgium to fear from Kossuth's presence? This is in full harmony with the spite then dominant in Austria.

All Europe seemed to Hungarian colonels to conspire against Hungary; therefore, alone perhaps, Görgey's treason prevailed. The Hungarian generals, when Görgey had exploded his ammunition, were honourably received by the Russian general; but when he had enticed as many as he could, he passed them over to the Austrians, who hanged them all. The Hungarian Premier, Batthyanyi, a man eminently loyal to Austria, had entered the Hungarian ranks in the character of a private soldier, as a patriotic protest; but before the war began in earnest, he went to Vienna as an ambassador of peace, in the hope of stopping bloodshed. Kossuth in vain dissuaded him. The Austrians at once arrested him, brought him to trial, and condemned him to long imprisonment. But when Görgey's treason had triumphed, they brought Batthyanyi to a second trial, and condemned him to be hanged. To avoid this ignominy, he slew himself, warning his son *never to trust Austria.* Such was the melancholy end of that memorable war.

Kossuth retired into Turkey. Pulszky had found his way to London, by mission from Kossuth. Among his early utterances to me was the following, in the close of 1849 :—" Our lot as exiles is hard. Possibly our countrymen, now under the Austrian heel, have a lot still harder; yet for a time only. The politics of Europe never remain long on the same footing. It is certain that a great change will take place in ten years, and Austria will greatly miss Hungarian energies. We have beaten her thoroughly, and *she knows it.* Her spite against us is intense, but she will never dare to fight us again. She will have to restore our hereditary laws, without any new war from us." First in 1859, then further in 1863, I had good reason to admire my friend's sagacity.

Russia and Austria both demanded of the sultan that he would give up Kossuth. The sultan had plentiful reason for dire vexation at the Russian invasion of Moldavia in 1848, and persistent violation of neutrality for passage into Transylvania. The Turks quickly understood how valuable an adviser Kossuth might be; and probably all thought that an enemy of Russia was their natural friend. Besides, the gallant victories of Hungary over Austria must have won their respect. In the American banquet given to Kossuth by the Houses of Congress, he glorified the noble conduct of the sultan, who had said, "I will accept war, rather than give up the Hungarian fugitives." Yet Kossuth himself told me, that he was not certain that the mild, kind, but timid 'Abd el Mejied would have had *courage* to resist the two emperors, had not Lord Palmerston argued for him as to treaty rights. Thus he frankly avowed that he possibly owed his life to Palmerston. The Austrians hanged both Kossuth and Pulszky *in effigy*. The latter had incurred their hatred by obeying the Hungarian Committee of Defence, when ordered to distribute in Vienna, by the thousand, copies of the treasonable despatch of the Austrian minister Latour to Jellachich. To this distribution the Austrians imputed the murder of Latour, with the second insurrection of Vienna, and blamed Pulszky for it, instead of blaming their own perfidy.

Kossuth, on crossing the Danube, sheltered by the Pasha of Widdin, at once set himself to learn the Turkish language, and with as excellent success as, in a cruel illegal Austrian captivity, he had learned English from Shakespeare and the English Bible some years before (1839). The Turkish Grammar which he now composed was soon after used (as I have read) in the common Turkish schools. Though the Hunnish race can produce such a man, it is disdained by pedantic Germans as collectively "Tartar and Gipsy."

HONOUR AND REPULSE AT MARSEILLES. 35

While still in Turkey he formed many acquaintances with patriotic Turks, and must have won much admiration and esteem. The sultan found Palmerston's advice wise, to pass the Hungarian exiles out of the country; but much liberality and honour accompanied the dismissal. Even England (as I *now* read) sent a ship to convey him away, but he preferred an American steamer, sent for him by the President. In September, 1851, it carried him to Marseilles, where he hoped to quit the sea, from which his wife's health suffered severely. The French of thát town received him with joy and triumph. *France was thén Republican;* but its heartless president, Louis Napoleon, was preparing murder on a great scale for the citizens whom he had sworn to protect; naturally he barred passage through France to Kossuth, whom the American steamer therefore dropped at Gibraltar. Thence he reached Southampton late in October, 1851.

While Kossuth was in England, he was slandered, feared, despised, and disliked by those

esteemed highest and noblest in England—
perhaps one nobleman called on him; but he
was enthusiastically received by the real nation.
He departed somewhat abruptly for America,
fearing quick events from St. Petersburg.
Before he could land on Staten Island (December 6) Louis Napoleon had already executed
his murderous raid on the French nation to
make himself despot of France. Panizzi, then
chief in the Library of the British Museum,
had been Napoleon's close friend during his
exile in England, and quickly went to Paris to
beg of his old comrade favours for *this and thát*
Frenchman, lovers of liberty, whose fortunes or
lives he feared might be attacked by Napoleon's
satellites. I heard Panizzi, on his return to
London, tell the tale of his success. Napoleon
received him with the utmost cordiality, and
with no ado granted him every favour which he
asked. "But what!" said one of those present. "When he was in exile here, he was
thought by many half-witted—almost a fool."
"A strong enthusiast, no doubt he was," re-

plied Panizzi ; "but certainly he has no want of talent ; and I was most agreeably astonished at his friendliness, perhaps gratitude, to me." "Well," asked another, "do you know how many he killed in thát *coup d'état*?" Panizzi was silent. Many guesses followed : 5000? 15,000? 20,000? Then at last Panizzi replied, "No register is kept. Napoleon himself is not likely to know, nor can he wish to know. Of course I cannot know; yet from what I do know ,I count 20,000 more likely to be *too few* than *too many*." Such was the estimate of a friend after friendly reception. Besides, numbers were sent as felons to Cayenne, a most unhealthy colony; many also were driven into exile. With such high-handed cruelties from royal and imperial aspirants, how wonderfully do royalists malign and slander republicans collectively, as eager for bloodshed !

When Pulszky was calmly recounting to me details of the Hungarian struggles, "Oh," I exclaimed, "this was *perfidious, atrocious,* of the Archduke Stephen !" He continued, quite unmoved, "Well, if you bring his conduct to the bar of our common morals, perhaps your words are not at all too severe. But then, you must remember"—he paused a moment, and then, slower and slower, added, with ever-increasing emphasis—"first of all, he *was*—an ARCH DUKE." Evidently he thought it *unfair* to expect "common morality" from such a quarter; and though the Austrians had stripped him of everything, and (against Hungarian law) had seized his wife's estate also, he seemed to cherish no personal resentment.

In America Kossuth was gloriously received. Here it suffices to state that in Boston (May, 1852) he elaborately set forth the certainty that Nicolas would lose no time to make war on Turkey. Meanwhile our Hungarian exiles naturally counted up Kossuth's errors of policy. Some thought *they* could have steered the ship of state better than he. Some of his honest coadjutors disparaged him as too mild—he ought to have arrested Görgey; and Austrian calumnies had spread widely. Moreover, the honourable part of the English press, and, no doubt, multitudes of his warmest wellwishers, after Louis Napoleon's successful usurpation, thought any new insurrection in Italy or Hungary sure to be fatal to the insurgents, and deprecated any English enthusiasm which might encourage false hope. *This made us appear fickle and cold.* In fact, the great cruelties of Austria became so unbearable in Milan, that an insurrection, deprecated by Mazzini, burst out in February, 1853; next, *in the hope of aiding* it, a fictitious address of Kossuth, calling on the Hungarians to rise simultaneously (the very opposite of Kossuth's advice) was published, and gained wide belief. Secret police had been set by the ministry of Lord Aberdeen (!) to dog Kossuth's movements; and during his change of residence his papers were seized by spies, and examined, under pressure from the Austrian ambassador. Nothing incriminating him could be found, but this conduct of our Executive struck into him like a dagger. He knew too well how Italian patriots had been sacrificed to Austrian policy in 1844, when Sir James Graham secretly opened Mazzini's letters, and betrayed to Austria their contents. Kossuth might have done nothing against English laws, but possibly much in his correspondence might expose some friend in Hungary to cruel attack from Austria, or damage his Turkish friends. He therefore earnestly desired that some friendly M.P. would exact of Aberdeen's ministry apology and clear explanation. A fierce and gratuitous attack was made on him concerning a certain Mr. Hale's rockets. Palmerston, who was now *Home* Secretary, was chiefly to blame; but he would neither exculpate Kossuth, nor attack him, nor apologize. His banter amused and silenced the House.

Palmerston may have been piqued, that no notice had been taken of the message by which he had given to Kossuth *unauthenticated* assurance that "he would like Kossuth to call on him." Kossuth explained to me his difficulty. "I cannot understand," said he, "what is the policy of Palmerston's *heart*. He talks one way, yet acts another way—always against the interests and just rights of Hungary. *If* his heart is with us, and some one behind has overruled him, I should naturally call and personally thank him; for *it may be* a fact, that his despatches to the sultan saved me from the Austrian gallows. Can you get for me, from any official who knows him well, a trustworthy, faithful account—what is his real character and policy?". The request was to me very embarrassing. At last I remembered one official whom I could dare to approach. This gentleman replied with gracious and ready frankness. " I have had many opportunities," said he, "of seeing into Palmerston's *wishes.* I cannot doubt that he desires our foreign policy to be liberal and just; and he will always act on that side, if he can do it without sacrifice to himself. But he has long believed that Nature has provided for England only two possible Foreign Secretaries, Aberdeen and Palmerston. That the latter should be displaced by the former he has regarded as *a European calamity*, so great that it is better for him to submit to do something which he disapproves, rather than lose office; which, indeed, for pecuniary reasons, I believe is quite unwelcome." This judgment I faithfully reported to Kossuth. In consequence, the latter, when plied with the question, "Why do you not call on Palmerston? *I am sure* he will be glad to see you;" replied only, "Really, I hardly know anything worth saying to Lord Palmerston; but if he has anything worth saying to me, and requests my presence, I will certainly obey his call." So thát matter ended; but Kossuth was increasingly uneasy, not only concerning his Hungarian, but perhaps more concerning his Turkish correspondence, which was probably by far the more continuous. The manifest hostility of the ministry and their courting of Austria, not only embittered him, but filled him with contempt for our policy, more and more when the Crimean war gradually rose on us. The tale is strange, and unknown to our younger people. I now approach it.

Young readers may be willing first to peruse

a paper, written by me in 1854, on "Russia and Turkey, and our *earlier* relations to Russia."

1854. "The present position of things cannot be well understood without some retrospect on the events which have happened since the last general war.

"In the peace of 1814-15 the large concession of our ministers to Russia did not escape the censure of the English Whigs. By what subtlety and threats the Emperor Alexander I., trimming between Napoleon and the allies, forced the latter to acquiesce in his seizure of Warsaw, was perhaps not publicly known before 1830; but it was quite clear that English policy had been unduly favourable to Russia, especially in eagerness to patch up the Russian title to Finland. To reconcile the new king of Sweden (Bernadotte) to the loss of this not inconsiderable part of his territory, Alexander engaged to indemnify him by the present of Norway; which was to be stripped from Denmark, a power against which the jealous policy of England had twice committed deadly wrong; therefore, apparently, having deserved hatred, our safest plan was, to weaken her. So eagerly did our Tories join in the Russian scheme, that when, after Danish assent had been extorted, the people of Norway refused to be bartered away, the English fleet was sent with the threat of blockading and starving them into submission. Such was the agency by which the French King of Sweden was reconciled to leave Finland in the grasp of Russia. Though Finland has been on the whole (I believe) generously and wisely treated, not trampled down as Poland, yet in the aggrandizement of Russia, England now learns the unwisdom of her injustice.

"All Europe, in fact, was cheated by the three Powers, whose union was enforced by Russian preponderance, and sanctified as the 'Holy' Alliance. The German people were defrauded of their historical union, and were persecuted by their own princes. The Italians and Sicilians were trampled down by Austrian force; the restored Bourbon in Spain overthrew the constitution which our Tories had approved;

another Bourbon in Naples, with Austria in the background, disowned the Sicilian constitution which the English fleet had aided to establish, for our safety against Napoleon. 'Your Tories *might* have saved their own handiwork in Sicily,' said our Continental critics, 'since Sicily is an island.' When, in 1820, great popular movements took place in Naples and Italy, as well as in Spain, Austrian armies first crushed the Italian patriots, and Russia behind gave Austria daring and confidence. Meanwhile, after France had gained eight years of repose, and her army was once more formidable, the Holy Alliance planned to use this new tool. In the Congress of Verona, Russian influence decided that the despotism of the Spanish king should be maintained, and the recent triumph of constitutionalism quelled by French invasion; a project which succeeded easily, when the traitor king was anxious for the invader's success. But this was the crisis at which the foreign policy of England changed for the better.

"Lord Londonderry, better known to us as Castlereagh, appears to have been overpowered by shame and vexation at the utter and manifest failure of his foreign policy in Sicily, in Spain, in Lombardy. He must have had intelligence of what impended from the Congress of Verona, and either yielded to a morbid mind or sank under insanity. His own penknife severed the great artery beneath his ear (1822), and virtually installed Mr. Canning as our Foreign Secretary instead of Governor-General in India. Against the Holy Alliance Canning displayed an indignation very rare in statesmen. He did not dare to give aid to Spain, but if our 'ally,' Portugal, were attacked, he threatened domestic revolution to the despots. The stamp of England's foot would arouse it! He certainly infused a new spirit into English diplomacy. Thenceforward England became the hope of the Continental patriots, while the despots regarded her as a power which may generally be managed and duped, but never can be friendly.

"To use his own proud boast, he resolved 'to raise in America a new world to redress the balance of the old.' He pressed strongly on President Monroe, of the United States, to issue a declaration, that if the European monarchs tried in favour of Spain to overthrow the republics there, which had risen out of Napoleon's conquest of Spain, 'such conduct would not be looked at with indifference by the American Republic.' This utterance, most unjustly and absurdly, is quoted by English newspapers as indicative of *American aggression;* but it was pressed on Monroe by Canning, who followed it up by admitting these republics into diplomatic relations with England.

"Yet apparently Canning himself, when at length Premier in 1827, became the dupe of Russian or French craft. Louis XVIII. of France, having ruled beneficially to France and constitutionally, died in September, 1824. His successor, Charles X., was eager to restore despotism in France, as it had been restored in Spain, by the grace of Russia, which was supposed to look favourably on the Greek rebellion against the intolerable yoke of Turkey. A French army was sent to occupy the Morea, the Peloponnesus of our school-days; Russia was at the same time threatening Moldavia. The Greeks could not sustain any regular army or fleet; of necessity their force was a *guerilla*, and their numerous small vessels were dreaded as *pirates* by European traders. Canning probably sympathized with the Greeks, but needed the argument, that since the sultan in five years could not suppress piracy in the Levant, collective Europe must do the work for him. Thus minded, Canning on this ground, and on this only, joined the other powers in what was then called the Treaty of London, not as a war against Turkey, but as a police measure against piracy. No war was declared or imagined; nevertheless, when the allied fleet sailed into the Bay of Navarino, where an Egyptian fleet, built to reconquer Greece, was at anchor, the Turkish admiral naturally accepted its approach as hostile; a battle ensued, and the sultan's fleet was annihilated. The chief force of the allies was English, next was the French. When the fatal news came to the Sultan Mohammed, his first care was to despatch horsemen to the towns in which most English or French were resident, with orders to the pashas to take instant measures for the protection of these foreigners from the hostility of the neighbouring Turks. Such facts from the Turks ought not to be forgotten by us.

"No doubt the Allies, who called themselves Mediators, were resolved to end the war of Greece, and (such had been the ferocity of the Turks against the Greeks of the island Scio) awoke by it great joy in all Europe. Yet the battle of Navarino, fought when Canning was just sinking into his grave, was deplored in the king's speech, with the Duke of Wellington as Premier, when it appeared that Russia alone was to be the gainer. Nicolas, who had become czar in 1825, at once declared war against Turkey, without any new grounds of war, and without laying aside the title (I believe) of

Mediator. The war was fought in 1828 and 1829, with enormous loss of Russian life in the capture of Danubian fortresses. When the victorious Russians at last reached Adrianople, their serviceable army consisted, in the highest estimate, of 13,000 men—some reduce it to 7000; but to the Turks the true number was unknown. The discouragement of the Turks was great, as the whole crisis had abounded with misfortune. The ambassadors counselled peace on the best terms to be got. Nicolas saw that it was wisest to be satisfied with the reality of power without its name; and peace was made at Adrianople. Under the Russian name, Count Capo d'Istria temporarily ruled Greece. Thenceforth, as is known from the secret despatches of Pozzo di Borgo, the czar has counted the sultan as his vassal. To Sir G. Hamilton Seymour he recently entitled him '*ce Monsieur.*'

"The defeat of the sultan in this war bore its usual fruit in making the pashas despise him. David, Pasha of Bagdad, immediately planned revolt, and withheld his usual tribute. He was too far off to attack instantly, and the sultan bore with his dissimulation for two years. In 1831 an expedition marched against him, which triumphed by aid of an awful plague in Bagdad and an inundation of the Tigris. The sultan's army captured an empty and ruined city. At the very same time Mohammed Ali Pasha of Egypt, who had for years trained his troops by French aid, even with a school for military art in drawing, conducted himself as a sovereign, and engaged in war against the Governor of Acre. In consequence, the sultan, in 1832, took up against him hostilities, which proved most disastrous to himself. The Egyptian army overran Syria with surprising ease. Indeed, Damascus had become hostile to the sultan from the violation of their local privileges, among which not the least valued was their right of various and degrading insult against Christians, even as to such matters as dress, and of riding so warlike an animal as a horse, instead of being content with an ass. Syrians in general, speaking Arabic, preferred an Egyptian ruler to one who talked the Ottoman language. Ibrahim Pasha, the Egyptian general, by the end of 1832 had reached Northern Syria, and when asked, 'How far are you going?' was reported to reply, 'As far as my Arabic will carry me.' However, he actually fought and conquered against an Ottoman army at Nezib, on the soil of Asia Minor. Lord Palmerston, then our Foreign Secretary, could not say, 'A strong *Turkey* is a European necessity;' but undoubted he believed that a very weak Turkey is a European calamity. The defenders of the Syrian war, which was begun and ended while Parliament was in recess, assure us that he knew as a certainty that the sultan, unless succoured by England or France against Ibrahim, would make petition to Nicolas for aid; therefore England must step in, to block Russia out (1840). Ibrahim moved back into Syria, and was expelled from the marine cities by the joint force of Turkish soldiers and English seamen. England established the fame of her paddle-steamers, and showed that the weakness of her navy was a Tory fantasy. The sultan, saved from his vassal by foreign aid, was humiliated and deeply weakened.

"But we must look back for ten years into France. Charles X., having captured Algiers in 1830, thought this exploit so dazzling to the French, that he might afford to break his coronation oath. Thereby he quickly lost his crown, and Louis Philippe succeeded him. The new king was unfaithful to Spain, but pursued a widely different policy toward Russia and Turkey. Russia indeed in 1831 had more than enough to do against the revolt of Warsaw, and was glad of aid from Prussia; but our Lord Grey, coming into power with the motto of 'Reform and Peace,' could not join Louis Philippe (and perhaps Austria) to re-establish the freedom of Warsaw. Thus Nicolas came out of that war with increase of military reputation. In 1833 he extorted from Turkey the new Treaty of Hankiar Skelessi, in which the sultan is bound to close the Dardanelles against every enemy of Russia. The French Premier (Thiers) was a zealot for Egypt, and most indignant with Lord Palmerston. Apparently, Louis Philippe saved himself and us from war by ejecting his Prime Minister and installing Guizot. But nothing could restore strength to the broken force of Turkey."

Re-approaching the Crimean war, the reader must remember that in February, 1848, Louis Philippe was driven out from Paris. France was proclaimed to be a Republic; in June the violence of socialists was crushed by General Cavaignac; Louis Napoleon was ere long elected President, and in 1851 in his turn crushed the Republic. Next year he made himself emperor.

The hectoring of French generals and colonels, natural to military men out of work, convinced French exiles in England that Napoleon would try to dazzle the French nation by "wiping out the disgrace of Waterloo;" an easy task, in their minds, if only their army could set foot on English soil. At Cherbourg, it was said, the emperor was collecting a powerful fleet. The alarm given by exiles was probably taken up by our military and naval men, always zealous for increased armaments. A noble earl in a London paper assured us that *if* the French army entered London on one side, the Guards would march out on the other. An eminent Italian commented to me, "In our certain belief not a single Frenchman would escape, except as a prisoner of war." But to us English that would be poor comfort for losses of life and ravage endured in subduing them. So general alarm increased. The ministry proposed to build for home-defence a new fleet, propelled (for the first time) by the Archimedean screw ; and Joseph Hume, stern economist as he was, went round in Parliament to his radical friends, imploring them to vote with the least possible delay the £600,000 required by the ministry, and do everything to expedite our security from French invasion. All Europe seemed crushed under three emperors, all bitterly hostile to English freedom. "By abandoning Hungary," said Kossuth, "you have brought danger to your own doors."

But our fear of Louis Napoleon was a fundamental mistake. His great desire was to win and keep the alliance of England. Palmerston courted him, quite prematurely; but Aberdeen, when Premier, dreaded him. Months passed, and when Napoleon discerned that the czar had designs far deeper than support of the Greek Church in Turkey against the Latin Church, he ordered the French fleet eastward to reassure the sultan; but Lord Clarendon (then become our Foreign Secretary in place of Lord John Russell), at once protested against it, and Napoleon submissively recalled the fleet. I am able to assert, that about this time, in reply to one who pressed on Lord Aberdeen that Napoleon was willing to send 50,000 men to Constantinople, where the Russian ambassador, Menzikoff, was making high demands on the sultan, Aberdeen exclaimed, " Fifty thousand Frenchmen! I would rather see 50,000 Russians there. When shall we get the French out of

Rome?" In the spring (perhaps April) of 1853 the *Times* newspaper, for a fortnight together, wrote leading articles in favour of dividing European Turkey between Russia and Austria. A friend of mine who had shares in the *Times* called on Mr. Walter, the chief proprietor, to remonstrate against these articles. Mr. Walter (he told me) replied, "I assure you I disliked them as much as you do; I yielded assent to them solely to please Lord Aberdeen." My friend proceeded, "I understand that Aberdeen argues thus: Nothing can now arrest the career of Nicolas but a coalition of England and France; but that is *morally impossible;* therefore it is best to accept the inevitable graciously." Looking back, it seems wrong to blame Aberdeen for thinking the coalition morally impossible; but in the actual result, the fleet built against Napoleon steamed in conjunction with the French fleet against the czar.

In midsummer, 1853, a Russian army crossed the Pruth and occupied Jassy. Moldavia, which from 1848 had for several years groaned under Russian extortions, was again crushed. The excitement in England was great; all now saw what came of the conquest of Hungary *for* Austria *by* Russia. The Austrian emperor had been closeted with the czar, who (according to *Punch*) pushed the bottle to him, saying, "Help me to finish the *Port.*" Men who had cared nothing for Hungary now saw that if Russia got into Constantinople, our instant reply would be, to double or triple our Mediterranean fleet. Nicolas, with an indefinite supply of Greek sailors, might be as powerful by sea as by land; collisions with him would be unavoidable, and if war arose, we should be *principals in it, without the aid of Turkey.* A debate in Parliament was vehemently desired, but the ministry sternly forbade, saying, "You will make a European war. Trust to us, and *we* will keep the peace."

To keep the peace, they planned a Conference at Vienna, with Francis Joseph as arbitrator, though they knew that Nicolas had said to our ambassador, Sir G. Hamilton Seymour, "Whatever I will, Austria wills." We seemed to him to be diligently playing his game, as in recalling the French fleet. It was not for nothing that in 1844 he had deposited a document in London to reveal his notions concerning Turkey; and of late he had unbosomed himself to Sir G. Hamilton Seymour, assuring him that the assent of England was all that he desired. In the Conference at Vienna our delegate pleaded so strongly against the Turkish interpretation of the Treaties, as to confirm the Russians in believing that no war could possibly come on them from England, "the land in which the doctrines of Cobden and Bright were dominant." Nesselrode therefore, the Russian Chancellor, resolving to push his advantage, declared that the *Turks were right*, and *the English wrong*, in their interpretation of the Treaties. This took the Western Powers quite aback, and broke up the Conference.

Meanwhile Kossuth, writing from London, had been instructing the Turkish statesmen on the ruinous consequences of conceding the claims of Russia, the temper of the English nation, the hollowness of the Cabinet, and, I believe, insisted that Right, Duty, Honour, and Expediency bound them to succour the oppressed Principalities, whose resources Russia was seizing as aids of her war. Our ambassador at Constantinople, Sir Stratford Canning, did his utmost to forbid the mild and gentle sultan from accepting the Russian war, but the ferment of the Turks became general. They avowed that the Western ambassadors were betraying them, and that in the name of peace they were being undermined by war. At length, in October, 1853, to the great mortification of our ministers, 'Abd el Mejied proclaimed war against Russia.

About this time, I believe, the Western fleets were sent first to Besika Bay, outside the Dardanelles; afterwards (with permission of the sultan) they went up to Constantinople itself. Her Majesty has fully set forth to us (what was not a public fact previously) that her Royal Consort in these months was a vehement promoter of war, and treated the peaceable desires of Lords Aberdeen and Clarendon as disgraceful. Hence, until better informed, we may infer that these movements of the fleets were *concessions to the prince*, though the bulk of the ministry abhorred the idea of actual war *for* Turkey *against* Russia. Palmerston alone advocated war, having learned in the case of Transylvania that Russia had (what he called) "two strings to her bow." A Russian general crosses a frontier; if the Powers are indignant at it, the move is disapproved at St. Petersburg as made without orders. But if the Powers take it calmly, the czar ratifies the deed, and seizes the advantage of it. So here, Moldavia is occupied, *not* (the czar informs us) *as an act of war*, but only "to obtain security for his diplomacy." Just so, argued Palmerston, a burglar establishes himself in your courtyard, to plunder you at his convenience. Before long Lord John Russell also seemed in Parliament to have warlike tendencies.

All the exiles—French, German, Italian, Hungarian—whom I met at that time in London, held one augury in common : " The next great war will be a war of Europe against Russia ; till that has been fought, there can be no security for law and liberty." Unjust institutions *will* cause war ; no Quaker talk or most earnest and righteous desire can avail to stop it while injustice rules. Had we mediated for Hungary, we should have saved Austria from the yoke of Russia, and have at least *put off* the Crimean war. But without some very severe shock Russia was not likely to unlearn baneful ambition, any more than England in India.

One morning Kossuth called suddenly on me with an English Blue-book in his hand, and abruptly said, " We foreigners look to you to explain your own Blue-books ; please to tell me, what does this strange sentence mean ? " I read carefully from the despatch of the Western Powers to the admirals of their fleets at Constantinople : " You must clearly understand that you are not sent to fight against the Emperor of Russia, but to save the sultan

INSTRUCTIONS TO OUR FLEETS. 63

from *religious enthusiasm and fatal auxiliaries.*" He pointed at these last words; I boggled over them. He presently burst into laughter, saying, "I see you do not understand them, and I must teach you. All Turkish patriotism necessarily has a religious tinge; therefore, *religious enthusiasm* is the diplomatic phrase for Turkish patriotism. *Fatal auxiliaries* mean Hungarians. Why so? Because Austria dreads lest exiled Hungarians fight in the Turkish ranks, and the object of the Western Powers is to please Austria, and not to aid Turkey. No, indeed! They are angry with the Turks for defending themselves against Russia, and send their fleet to save the sultan from the brave patriotism of his own people! To save Austria from Hungary is the main effort of your ministers."

I afterwards saw that Lord Clarendon, in commenting on Sir G. H. Seymour's secret despatches, had dissuaded the czar from attacking Turkey just now, lest certain great Powers should be exposed to danger from insurgents, to whom they had recently proved unequal;

which meant, lest a Turko-Hungarian alliance be the ruin of Austria.

How unjust in 1848–54 were even our Whigs was typically shown by Mr. Macaulay. I venture here to quote a part of a speech, prepared by me at the request of the Polish Committee for November 29, 1854, on the oppressed Nationalities. *Time* then cut me short, through the eagerness to hear Kossuth.

"As I was strongly urged to take part this evening, in the hall where you commemorate and anticipate Polish independence, I felt unable to refuse, although I have little claim to address the present company.

"I know nothing of Poland beyond what is on the surface of history. I can only speak of Poland as part of the great European question. That conspiracy of despots against national freedom which Lord John Russell in Parliament confessed to exist, has made the cause of Poland, Bohemia, Hungary, Croatia, and Italy, to be but one cause; and they are all essentially included in the anti-Russian movement.

"That I may not be mistaken, permit me to say, that I do not venture to blame our ministry for not having landed troops on the coast of Courland and called the Poles to arms. I am aware that the Emperor of the French must have a voice in such a question, and the King of Prussia also will claim one. For allies to agree in the conduct of a war, is notoriously difficult. . . .

"But on one broad fact I first desire to lay stress, that from 1849 to 1854 our aristocracy have fallen into a grievous illusion, an unjust blunder, a disastrous infatuation, in confounding the righteous and necessary movements of European nationalities against lawless oppression with the wayward and fitful proceedings of the mere populace of Paris. I will quote from a man, whom I name for honour, but who nevertheless is, by reason of his eminence, a type of this disastrous blunder: I mean Mr. Macaulay. Our ministers are (by a sort of fatal necessity hitherto) either Tory or Whig, or mixed of both; and no one will say that the Tory side has been *more* favourable to European liberty and national rights than the Whigs; while among the Whigs there is no man who has been in conscience and in intention a firmer and braver friend to liberty than Mr. Macaulay. No one among them is so broad and deep in his knowledge, so keen in his logic, so brilliant and various in his talents, so consistent in his politics, so thoroughgoing in his arguments, so unflinching an enemy to the lawless usurpations of princes. I really believe that his recent volume of Speeches compares with any similar production in literature; and *will* compare, until our illustrious friend, Mr. Kossuth, shall find leisure in some distant year to collect and edit a small selection from his countless speeches. Well, I quote Mr. Macaulay—personally, I say, for honour, yet as exhibiting the disastrous blunder committed by Whigs and Tories collectively. In his speech delivered on his re-election to Parliament, at Edinburgh, November 2, 1852, he propounded it as a fact, that in the conflicts of 1848-9, not in France only, but in *Germany, Hungary, Italy,* THE KINGS WERE

FIGHTING IN THE CAUSE OF CIVILIZATION, AND THE NATIONALITIES WERE RISING TO DESTROY IT, IN THE CAUSE OF ANARCHY. This he actually spoke, after our Blue-books of Hungary and Italy had come forth. Allow me to read you a passage, pp. 505, 506:—' For myself, I stood aghast [at the popular movements]; and though naturally of a sanguine disposition, I did for one moment doubt whether the progress of society was not about to be arrested, nay, to be suddenly and violently turned back; whether we were not destined to pass in one generation from the civilization of the nineteenth to the barbarism of the fifth century. I remembered that Adam Smith and Gibbon had told us that the dark ages were gone. . . . It had not occurred to them that civilization itself might engender the barbarians who should destroy it. It had not occurred to them, that in the very heart of great capitals, *vice and ignorance* might produce a race of Huns, fiercer than those who marched under Attila, and of Vandals more *bent on destruction* than those who followed

Genseric. SUCH WAS THE DANGER. It passed by. CIVILIZATION WAS SAVED. But at what a price!'——

"Here is gratuitous calumny—from such a man! Even as applied to Paris, it is an unjust exaggeration. No wanton slaughter or *destruction* was committed by the populace in the three days of February, 1848, and no sooner had they won the republic, than they sternly defended property and life, abolished capital punishment, and attacked no man for his opinions or suspected tendencies. They brought back the dangerous Bonapartes, so trusting were they. It has been everywhere the reactionary party that perpetrate imprisonments and murders in time of peace, but not the people. But was it *vice and ignorance* which led to the insurrection of Sicily and of Milan against their barbarous oppressors? Was it anarchy which led the Romans to enact a well-ordered government, when the Pope ran away, and for ten weeks left them to anarchy, and returned to imprison the flower of his country? There *was* indeed barbarism;—the King of Naples let loose convicts to assassinate, and gave free leave of pillage to beggars—there *was* infuriation of race against race, as Mr. Macaulay complains; but it was stirred up by the wickedness of the Hapsburgs, who armed rude Serbs and Croats against the peaceable and trusting Hungarians, burnt the villages, slaughtered the unarmed people, yet denounced the ·marauders, ordered the Hungarians to arm against them, and then treacherously commanded the generals to fight a sham battle against the rebels, and allow the Hungarians to be defeated. The broad facts were notorious two full years before Mr. Macaulay spoke thus; yet he accuses the *people* of that barbarism which belonged solely to those whom the wicked princes suborned, used as their tools, and finally cheated of their hire. Anarchy! I would fain ask Mr. Macaulay whether Louis Batthyanyi was an anarchist? or in what point he was morally or legally inferior to Mr. Macaulay's heroes, our Hampden and Pym. Louis Batthyanyi went as an ambassador of peace, with a flag of truce, to the Austrian camp, in the hope of averting civil war. He was treacherously arrested; he was tried by court-martial and sentenced to imprisonment; he was kept in prison till the war was over, was then *again* tried by court-martial, for alleged offences purely civil, when a civil court might have been held; finally he was sentenced to be hanged, and evaded such a death by his own sword. . . . Mr. Macaulay cannot deny that Austria and Russia, who trampled down Hungary, are alike ruthless and lawless; nothing of this kind can be laid against the Hungarian nation, any more than against Poles or Italians. What then does he mean by pretending that these two usurping forces are the champions of civilization? Civilization! Why, our very Tories of the *Quarterly Review* and *Blackwood's Magazine* have made the discovery, that the present war is one for Civilization against Barbarism, and that the Czar of Russia is the barbarous power. When did he first become so? Was he different, when he crossed the Pruth in

1853, from what he was in 1848, when he took the same violent step?"

The duplicity of our ministers, which entangled us in the war, apparently arose from the contrary zeal of H.R.H. the Prince Consort *for* war, and of the ministry *against* it; while secret diplomacy veiled their doings and their objects. Yet it remains obscure, that so honourable a man as Lord Aberdeen could possibly sanction such a fraud on the sultan, as to send a fleet *as if* to support him, and *forbid* the admiral to act. I *suppose* he reconciled himself to it, on the positive promise of the czar, which was undoubtedly given (Lord Palmerston dwelt on it in Parliament) that *if* the sultan confined the war to the Principalities, so would the czar. Even so, our ambassador, Sir Stratford Canning, may seem *not to have been informed* of the instructions to the admirals; for in December, 1853, he introduced Admiral Dundas and others in solemn divan to the sultan, with these words, "Your Majesty, these are the chief officers of the fleet, whom the queen, my mistress, *has sent to defend you* from unjustifiable aggression." Some ten days later the sultan desired to reinforce certain garrisons on the north coast of the Black Sea, and was about to send his war ships to convoy his transports ; but Sir Stratford was believed to forbid it, saying, "The ships of war will be attacked, and this will make a European war ; but the Russians will not attack mere transports. They will go safe ; for the czar has engaged not to extend war beyond the Principalities." Nevertheless, the Russian admiral interpreted the reinforcing of garrisons to be an extending of the war into the Black Sea, and utterly destroyed the helpless transports with Paixhan shells, then (I believe) for the first time used. This "massacre of Sinopè" made the war inevitable. The sultan called on the admirals to avenge him on the Russian fleet, and they had no choice but to confess that *they were forbidden* to do so. How treacherous were his allies, the sultan could no longer deny, and all the most *patriotic* Turks, friends of Kossuth, succeeded to chief influence.

That Napoleon was smitten to the heart by this disgrace, he himself avowed some three months later, in his autograph letter to the czar, pitifully representing and deploring the danger of a war, easily avoidable, if both sides were wise in time. With that letter before me, Mr. Kinglake will never persuade me that Napoleon desired war. He felt intensely the disgrace of treachery incurred by the massacre of Sinopè, with the two Western fleets inactive. (Visibly to the Turks, Western aid was dangled before their eyes as a mere bait, to hinder their taking the course that self-defence suggested.) We now feel (says Napoleon), not a mere defeat of our diplomacy, but a stain on our honour. Only in one way could war now be averted. Let the Russian armies go back to their own side of the Pruth, and let the Western fleets return into the Mediterranean; then diplomacy can resume its normal career.

Nicolas, no doubt, was intensely disgusted to find that England was likely to join with Napoleon against him, after all his efforts to please us, and all the favour shown him by our ministry. Incensed pride may have aided to make him obstinate. Yet his obstinacy may not have had its chief source in resentment; it is almost certain to me now that he made a very pacific reply, and that the two allies received it in a like spirit, for it soon leaked out that he assured them of his earnest desire for peace the moment he could propose it without dangerous loss of *prestige*. In fact, he had been at war with Turkey along the Danube from October to March or April, had sustained many severe repulses, and had not been able to win a single small success against the *unaided* Turks, whom he had expected to defeat and trample down quickly. How terrible then to him the prospect of encountering France and England as their allies! Soon after it oozed out that we counted on his making peace *after his first plausible success*. Probably this was his secret answer to Napoleon's autograph letter. On this came Clarendon's celebrated confession in the House of Lords, that we seemed to be "drifting" into war.

A SHAM WAR.

But our too clever ministry, which had dreaded frank and timely speech in Parliament, and believed in Secrecy as the talisman of Peace, had not yet exhausted its store of duplicities. War was declared against Russia with due formality. Pulszky first, on telling me that Lord Raglan was to lead 10,000 men against the armies of Russia, scoffed at so small a force, but next day brought the strange news that Lord Raglan had pleaded for 25,000, not as adequate *for fight*, but as better proportioned *to his honour* as Field Marshal, and he was to have 26,000. A few days later a friend asked me whether I could believe what he was told, that Lord Raglan, when waiting with many others for admission to the queen's levee, had loudly said, "Do not be alarmed, any of you; we shall not fire a single shot in the East." I had no reply to give; but about a week later a copy of the Parisian *Galignani* fell into my hands, in which certain words caught my eye: "Lord Raglan recently passed through Paris, and caused great excitement by repeating, 'We shall not fire a single shot in the East.'" On reading this, I believed. It was presently confirmed by something stranger still. Though we had declared war, Mr. Gladstone, then Chancellor of the Exchequer, asked of Parliament money to carry the troops *to Malta and back;* a formula much commented on in England and soon circulated in Russia. However, our army did not stick in Malta. It did reach Turkish soil, but sat idle near to a marsh against which David Urquhart had warned us as pestilential. Neither the French nor English army ventured near to the scene of battle, where the Russians, after many repulses from Omar Pasha (a skilful Austrian who had accepted Islam), were concentrating their efforts against the town of Silistria on the Danube. Omar sat idle with his main army at Shumla, and the strange report prevailed, that the Western ambassadors forbade him to succour Silistria; which, according to the *Times* newspaper, was almost day by day expected to fall. I cannot remember when and where first leaked out the confident assertion that Nicolas had promised us to make peace as soon as he had established his military credit; and *that* was why the allies of Turkey *forced* the Grand Vizier to hold back Omar Pasha.

But I am forgetting another episode at the opening of this war, of which we did not at all understand the meaning at the time. After declaring war, the first necessary act of prudence with our ministry was, to shut up the two principal Russian fleets in their narrow seas. Our Mediterranean fleet at Besika Bay had already secured us from their passage through the Dardanelles, and with all speed a second fleet was sent to the Baltic under Sir Charles Napier, the admiral so celebrated in Lord Palmerston's Syrian war. Sir Charles imagined that his exploits at Acre and Alexandria were to be repeated against Cronstadt, or possibly against St. Petersburg itself. He had no notion that his duty was the tame one of blocking the narrows at Copenhagen against the passage of the Russian fleet. He sent round a vivid message to the crews of all his ships, bidding them to sharpen their cutlasses for boarding * the Russian ships at Cronstadt. He cannot have been aware that his ships rode too deep in the water to get within shot of Cronstadt; and, to his grave mortification, a sharp public reproof came back to him from Sir James Graham, then Secretary (I think) of the Admiralty, bidding him to "*run no risk* with ships or men"—a very novel injunction to a dashing and successful English admiral. Whether Sir James Graham at that time was aware how shallow is the sea round Cronstadt, I cannot say; gunboats of light draught were built for approach, *too late for the war*. In retrospect we at length understand that the Aberdeen ministry intended no actual fight in the Baltic; and certainly the idea of bombarding St. Petersburg (if it had been in our power), was horrible. But, as I now believe, Nicolas had already promised "to confine his war to the Principalities," and our rulers were resolved

* *Bord* (side) is not *board*.

not to strike him in the Baltic, though they dared not leave the "*Belts*" unguarded.

Unluckily for the Western intrigue, two English officers, returning from India, passed through Turkey, and threw themselves into Silistria, the besieged town. Their zeal, counsels, and activity gave new life to the defenders; perhaps also were mistaken for a foretaste of English brave support. Under the new energy —most provoking to Russia, England, and France—Silistria continued impregnable. The *Illustrated London News*, a paper written for Tories and Whigs of the well-to-do classes, was shocked at the aspect of things, and wrote some instructive eye-opening paragraphs concerning it. The *Times* newspaper seemed impatiently to desire the fall of Silistria.

Meanwhile, intrigue from the Austrian Cabinet was active. It desired some "finger in the pie" as a plea for "annexation." Austrian policy was eager to occupy something. Servia, then a dependency of Turkey, had received local self-government, and was quite loyal; but Austria requested of the Western Powers authority to occupy Servia—forsooth, against Russia, in the interests of the sultan. But the Servian Executive protested so intensely, that neither France nor England could decently assent. I never saw the actual words in any newspaper, but only in the Sheffield speech (June 5, 1854) of Kossuth, who, no doubt, had all from Reshid Pasha, to whom they were addressed. They deserve prominence. "Even admitting that the Russians should attempt to enter Servia, any auxiliary force would be preferable to that of Austria. The Servian nation entertain so great a distrust, not to say pronounced hatred, of Austria, that the whole action of the Servians would be turned against the Austrian force, an enemy in whom is beheld the personification of a grasping ambition." In spite of this rebuff, our ministers (including Lord John Russell!) longed to entice Austria from the side of Russia; but took care to warn her, that her Italian provinces were open to our attack, if she imprudently joined Russia against us.

She presently did great service to Russia, and we did not resent it. The Servian Diet voted 70,000 troops to aid the sultan against his invader; but the Austrians in reply placed an army of 90,000 to invade Servia, and forced her to keep her own troops at home for self-defence, thus depriving the sultan of 70,000 brave men. Indeed, for four years back the conduct of Austria had shown the Turks her enmity, and that she was sure to join Russia against them as soon as she dared.

The Western allies still tried to please Austria; and when she soon after proposed to occupy Bulgaria in the interest of the sultan, they gave a favourable reply. "Why so," was for me, at the time, a great mystery. I afterwards solved it to myself, as follows:—They believed that Russia was certain, at length, to capture Silistria, and from it they argued that she would surely conquer all Bulgaria north of the Balkan. Once there, how could she be expelled? She might claim to make peace, but would keep the province; and then take her own time for moving into Constantinople. But if we now brought Austria in, Austria would not dare to aspire to that prize, and was far easier to be controlled than Russia; meanwhile she would keep Russia out.

Perhaps such was the *motive* of the Western Powers; but as soon as they opened the scheme to the Grand Vizier, they found him intensely obstinate against it, and were driven to play their last card, by claiming from the weak sultan to dismiss him and replace him by another in whom we trusted, having known him as ambassador in London. But the new Vizier was no fool. He knew that, having ejected his predecessor, we could not so easily eject him; he therefore, in yielding to our pressure for the admission of Austria, insisted on the condition that Omar Pasha, who was now kept inactive at Shumla, should be allowed (!) to succour the sultan's garrison in Silistria. The allies no longer had impudence enough to forbid it. Then followed the result, *hei, presto!* like a magical trick. Omar Pasha's arrival soon drove off the Russians and freed

Silistria; but the Austrians descending the Danube interposed, and hindered the Turks from pursuit of the fugitive Russians. In this way *those* very regiments escaped, which, in the prolongation of the war, all but crushed our English force at *Inkermann*.

Thus the czar could not *recover "his prestige"* and dared not make peace, much as he and England and France wished it. Here truly was a state of things for others beside Quakers to mock or curse, or both—three great nations all fighting against their will, solely because none of them had known how formidable a defence, under a skilful general like Omar Pasha, the south bank of the Danube formed. All through this first campaign the Western war was a sham. We did not defend our nominal ally; we wished success to our nominal enemy. We were vexed that our ally fought so successfully; and now (as Lord John Russell afterwards declared) we did not know what else to do, but to attack in earnest the Russian stronghold of Sebastopol.

I asked of a young English officer, just returned from India, whether he had any opinion *how* we ought to deal with that peculiar fortress? He answered with the gravity of a sage. "If you *will* undertake such wars," said he, "you must lose life—lose hundreds of lives; but the shorter the war, the fewer; and you must sometimes run great risks. But, in my opinion, we shall take Sebastopol with least loss by our fleet dashing boldly in. The batteries on both sides at worst might cost us two or three ships, with their crews; but the rest would make sure capture of the Russian fleet; then the harbour and forts would be ours." While he spoke, Prince Gorchakoff had already sunk the whole Russian fleet in the harbour, in dread of our betaking ourselves to this mode of attack! It may seem that, to conquer in war, the commander's prudence must not outweigh his enterprize.

This Russian war was continued, more signally than any war known to me, simply *on the mere point of military honour.* The allies were ashamed of their inaction, Russia was ashamed of having been repulsed.

But I have omitted a curious episode, and must go back to what took place before we had *declared* war in April, 1854, when the Turkish ministry despaired of faithful aid from allies so unfaithful, though the feeble-minded sultan was not equal to the occasion. Kossuth called on me, and said, "This is a great crisis for me; the sultan's war-minister summons me to Constantinople, where I am to sign the treaty of alliance, offensive and defensive, between Turkey and Hungary. I tell you this, for the chance that you may suggest my quickest way towards getting £5000. I should dishonour my country in the eyes of the Turks, unless I appear in a steamer on which I can raise the Hungarian flag, and am surrounded by a few officers in uniform. This, I find, may be done by £5000, barely by less." I was confounded; but, after a little thought, I said, "My advice is very feeble; but such as it is, I must give, at your request. I know a printer who is a zealot for Hungary, and keeps on file copies of all the papers which contain your great English speeches. I think he may be able to pick out the names and addresses of the richest men who spoke vigorously on the side of Hungary. If he will do his best, I advise you to write a circular for him to send to these select names. Let your circular be very short, and to this effect: 'A sudden crisis emboldens me to approach every one who approves the just cause of Hungary, and can afford to aid it by money, and can trust my honour and patriotism. I ask him to contribute as much as his heart and his means dictate. I want £5000 immediately.'" He thanked me, and departed. A little later, I asked what had been his success. He replied, "I sent out a circular such as you suggested. I wanted £5000 and got about £400; but I am glad I did not get more. All is right." I begged him to explain. Then he said, "I have since received a new despatch from the Selikhdâr, earnestly hoping that his letter will come in time to stop me. He tells me, that your ambassador, by bribes irresistible to poor underlings, wormed out the secret that a document had been prepared for my signature. Thereupon Lord Stratford demanded a secret conference with the sultan, *tête-à-tête*, excluding all the sultan's ministers. What threats or what promises he used, can only be guessed; but he obtained from the sultan, in entire ignorance of the sultan's Cabinet, a promise that if Kossuth returned to Constantinople, he should be sent to a fortress and kept prisoner there." So far Kossuth drily told me the facts: then, rising majestically, uttered some eloquent and more impassioned words, which I cannot reproduce accurately; but their substance was this: "Your ministers write despatches to instruct us foreigners—oh, how wisely and beautifully; but when an Oriental prince takes a feeble step in your virtuous direction, seeking to avoid by a publicly notified and select ministry THE EVIL OF PERSONAL RULE, *this*, *this* is the way" (rapping sharply on the table with his manuscript) "that you teach him to govern constitutionally."

Kossuth darkly alluded to these affairs in the Nottingham Music Hall, June 12, 1854. "The Western Powers," said he, "fawning upon Austria, had stipulated with the sultan that 'no Hungarian officer be admitted to Omar Pasha's army, and that Kossuth be hindered—by open force, if necessary—to land in Turkey,' though the Turkish people often called loudly for him." Probably ever since the massacre at Sinopè in the preceding winter, all Turks had despaired of Western good faith. Still worse, when, after seeing Austria deprive the sultan of 70,000 Servians, these nominal allies continued to court her, and made secret stipulations at her request with the sultan in spite of his constitutional advisers. These doings, I presume determined the Turkish ministry to send for Kossuth. But the sultan was overpowered by the hope of alliance, which we sold to him at so dear a price, never imagining what price we ourselves would have to pay.

The English nation from beginning to the end of these affairs was resolute and patient. From the moment that they understood the helplessness of Austria and the ambition of Nicolas (that destroyer of Hungarian freedom), they decided that the career of Russia *must be arrested*. The wonderful matter, in retrospect, is, the great alarm of Aberdeen's Cabinet lest Hungarian blood rather than English should be shed to restrain Russian ambition. To avoid this, they first blundered into disgraceful fraud by sham alliance, next (against their own fixed purpose) entangled themselves in war. When will England insist on depriving her ministers, and thereby her officers, from making war without previous public debate and judicial approval? Ministers who dreaded firm words from Parliament which would certainly have controlled the cautious Nicolas, enticed him to enterprize by their flatteries, and believed that they alone could keep the peace.

Mr. Gladstone, with Lord Aberdeen and others, we now learn, had a *conscience* against upholding the Ottoman power, because long experience proved that in the most vital matters it could not do justice to its Christian subjects. Why then was not this argument laid before our Parliament, when so widely spread a movement pleaded for aiding the sultan? On the contrary, debate in Parliament was gagged. We knew that Servia (professedly Christian) was eager on the sultan's side, also to the two Danubian Principalities the sultans had always been just and faithful ; while Russia (at least since 1848) was very oppressive, and the Christians on that area looked to the Turks for aid. Lord Palmerston, against the imputation of Mohammedan bigotry, avowed that " it would be well for all free religionists in Naples or Rome or Russia " (my memory is uncertain as to all the areas named by him) "if they could have the same toleration as from the sultan. Hungarians asserted, that in past centuries many Protestants took refuge under the Turks from the bigotry of their Austrian kings. Kossuth also has testified to the honourable dealing of the sultans to the two Principalities. Evidently, while Christian Powers are unjust in bigotry—not least Russia—Mr. Gladstone's topic cannot be fitly pleaded against the sultan. Nevertheless, it remains sadly true that where Christians and Mohammedans are mingled, no sultan has power to control occasional, perhaps outrageous, fanaticism of his Turks. Therefore, if for any Christian district we can gain escape from Turkish supremacy, without casting it under Austrian or Russian bigotry, we may rejoice.

It occurred to me to speculate, if, when Nicolas held his frank conference with Sir G. H. Seymour, *Cobden*, instead of Lord *John Russell*, had been Foreign Secretary, how would he have dealt with the case? To Cobden I never could look up, though there was plenty in him to applaud; but after his wild utterance in the City of London Tavern, that he could crumple up Russia like the sheet of paper in his hand, I could not desire him to replace Lord John Russell. Nevertheless, I believe his sterling honesty would have done for us the needful work. He would have said to the czar (through Sir G. H. Seymour), "We have too much to do in Ireland and India and the Colonies, besides home work, to imagine that we can wisely undertake to revise and regulate the action of Russia towards her neighbours. Her Majesty's present advisers may be depended on as consistently pacific. Nevertheless, we emphatically warn his Russian Majesty, that if it be believed in England that he is moving towards the conquest of Constantinople, or to such a predominance over the sultan as to be able to dispose of the Dardanelles as his own, a frenzy of war *will sweep us pacific men out of office*, and no promises of past ministries will be of any avail to hinder the entire force of England from being directed against the czar." Cobden's blunt honesty would have repressed the ambition of Nicolas, as efficiently as Lord John Russell's smooth flattery inflamed it.

Lord Aberdeen and his associates, when their sham war had proved futile, and the earnest war, *which their conscience condemned*, confronted

them, ought, I believe, to have resigned *at once.*
It would have been a grievous humiliation, yet,
I think, better than waiting for disaster to
make them resign. The disaster came from
ill-arranged duties and want of practical knowledge; very possibly also from appointments
having been made in a blind expectation that
the war would be a sham. In Russian estimate,
our private soldiers were lions led by asses.
Winter was a more impartial judge than
Russians, as to the capacity of our storemanagers. Thick coats and fur boots and every
appliance of need or possible luxury had been
sent from England without stint, and were safely
housed either at Constantinople or at Balaklava. Our troops, after the two victories of
Alma and Inkermann, were on the tableland
of Sebastopol, within six miles of Balaklava,
with no enemy between, yet were perishing by
frost and famine. The general-in-chief was
diligènt to furnish them abundantly with shot
and shell; but, somehow, no one thought of
clothing, food, and tents, nor of marching

regiments down one at a time, to procure the necessaries of life for themselves; while mules, it was said, were unequal to the road ploughed up by the weight of ammunition. No one seemed to know where to find anything, or *who* might dare to break open a package. This heartbreaking starvation (as Lord John Russell called it) of our brave and victorious army caused the resignation of Aberdeen and the bulk of his Cabinet.

In the course of these distressful events the Prince Consort uttered an oracle very enigmatic: "Now it will be seen how a *free* nation can conduct a great war." Was perhaps the true meaning nearly as follows :—" Louis Napoleon, a despotic prince, has not blundered as we have. If England had been *less free*, and I had had the management here, as Napoleon in France, oh, how much better would things have gone!" But such interpretation is conjectural.

Palmerston became Premier of a new ministry. He sent out the whole material and appliances for a six-mile railway to join Balaklava to the battlefield, and continued the war vigorously. It was no longer to be a sham. The Turks were to see that the Western Powers were in earnest. Gunboats were at once to be built, shallow enough to approach Cronstadt. An Anglo-French fleet was sent to the Pacific to attack the Petro-Paul fortress, and block Russian ships from coming down on our distant colonies. Now also, it seems, Napoleon must have matured his scheme of sheathing ships with iron, which in the next year he used with full success against Russia at Kertch, and, if I do not mistake, against her batteries at Kherson. It was the beginning of our too-famous ironclads. The Western Powers *in no case* joined their forces with those of the sultan, who, nevertheless, sent an army into Eupatoria, in the Crimea. Here, again, the Russians attacked them, only to meet with repulse. This was as the last straw to the camel's back. The great ambitious czar, who had expected to trample down the despised Turk, had met with nothing but failure from them. It was too much for his nerves, though they seemed to be of brass; so he broke his heart and died.

Lord John Russell had imagined that to win Austria to our side was a great point. A like futile attempt to win the aid of Prussia was made from a leading Tory lord (Lyndhurst) by insane invective. The two Powers conterminous to Russia had far more to lose by attacking her, than we Western Powers who fought from safe distance; they would not pull "our chestnuts out of the fire" with their own fingers. Palmerston sent Lord John to Vienna, as ambassador extraordinary, to work out his problem. Lord John was so stung with dismay by his cold reception, that he advised to beg peace from Russia on Russian terms. But the English nation regarded this as a new cheating of the sultan and a fatal aggrandizing of Russia. Not a single popular complaint had been made of the vast expenses of the war; and its awful mismanagement caused only deep grief. But as the late Sir Charles Trevelyan avowed, he never before so much honoured and valued the temperament of our English people, who were proved moderate but firm; the same in success or in hardship and doubtful fortune. Their steadiness kept the ministers steady. Palmerston did his utmost to hinder Parliament from affixing the blame of frightful mismanagement on any individual. We were to be satisfied by the verdict that the *system* was to blame! (How much is the system altered now?) But at least Palmerston continued the war, and planned to continue it beyond what Napoleon thought prudent. Early in 1856 the Emperor Alexander II. obtained *his first success* in the capture of the city of Kars, in Armenia, and at once proposed peace. He submitted to yield up the historical fortress of Ismail (which now, being in the Dobrudscha, belongs to Roumania), to be shut out from even the northernmost mouth of the Danube (which the Russian czars had used very wrongfully), and to make engagement to keep no ships in the Black Sea on the scale of a war fleet. Thus Constantinople seemed safe. In 1870, when France was at war with Germany, the czar, Alexander II., disgracefully repudiated the last condition. Such conduct tends to make treaties waste paper; yet in extenuation we must note, that he did not *actually* build a war fleet in the Black Sea, but in her recent war with Turkey, Russia was inferior in marine to the sultan, both on the Danube and on the Black Sea.

To give any details of the war of Sebastopol could not be in place here; but I may dwell on the consequences of the war, which the Quakers ever since have been asserting to have been *wholly futile.* From the battle of Waterloo to the Crimean war all went for the worse on the European continent, except to France; of this mischief Russian superiority was the chief cause. The "Holy Alliance" ruined the free constitutions of Spain and of Sicily, set up by aid of English Tory ministers. Russia in the background sustained Austrian despotism in Northern Italy, and Austria sustained Neapolitan despotism. In Germany, Austria was too powerful against Prussia. But the Crimean war forced Russia out of the field for some ten years, and in the interval thus gained, Italy first was united under a popular constitutional king; next Prussia became head of Germany; after this, Austria was forced to reconcile herself to Hungary, and became soundly constitutional. Thus Europe has now, as bulwarks against Russia, two first-rate military Powers —an abundant security. Both of them are moderately progressive and peaceful, now happily joined by Italy as guardians of peace. Only by some very severe blow dealt to Russia could these results have been achieved. A first-rate war to check her was a *sine quâ non*.

It is time now to pass to my other topic— from the Crimean to the Franco-Austrian war. Between the two were barely three years, yet some retrospect is needful to clear up the springs of the latter war.

Louis Napoleon, as Prince President of the French, obtained from Lord Palmerston in 1850 English approval to restore the pope to Rome "under an improved Government." The pope,

Pius IX., who began his reign in 1846 by the liberal act of releasing State prisoners, and by other deeds which made Mazzini dream that in him Italy would find a real deliverer, quickly revealed his true self, when Italy made effort to throw off the Austrian yoke. Terrified by the assassination of a high officer who had earned the public hatred, the pope, in November, 1848, secretly fled from Rome to Gaeta (a maritime Neapolitan city), and refused three successive respectful deputations, entreating him to return. At last the Romans, to terminate anarchy, enacted a Provisional Government, and gathered votes from every district as to the form of the future rule. France was at that time a Republic, and was acknowledged as such by England and other Powers. In the Papal territories a Constituent Assembly of 150 members, in February, 1849, enacted a Triumvirate (that is, a Supreme Cabinet of three men), and abolished the Temporal Papacy. The three men who thus became *joint presidents* were Mazzini, Saffi, and Armellini. All was done with peace and strict legality; but the Catholic kings of Naples and of Spain were resolved to overthrow the new Republic. Palmerston knew also that Austria would not endure it, and probably believed he did kindly for Rome by assenting to its occupation by France, with the restoration of the pope "under an improved Government." He afterwards expressed horror at the terrible carnage, and explained that *he had not expected the Romans to fight!* A year of noble struggle had awakened the national spirit. Ferdinand Lesseps, then French consul in Rome, warned his president that the French army would have to leave the noblest Romans dead on the pavement; but Napoleon did not care, and Palmerston did not believe. Napoleon's bloodshed restored the pope, but earned no gratitude from him. The pope would not hear of an improved Government, nor of lay predominance. Napoleon could not fulfil his promise to our ministry, and presently found his life exposed to the Italian dagger as his sole reward. To divert such attacks, he tried to pass himself off as leader of "the Nationalities" against Austria, who was the sworn foe of national claims, and, wonderful as it may seem, he now tried to entice Kossuth into his following. Kossuth revealed to me the fact, probably in 1853; of this I shall presently speak further. But how sad is the charge which Italy made against even an English *Whig* ministry! Napoleon I., in September, 1801, suppressed the temporal power of the Pope, delivered Northern Italy from clerical rule, which was always crippling and exclusive; he had ruled Italy, both north and south, by Italian natives; hereby he developed the national spirit. But when he fell by his own grasping ambition, the allies punished Italy, by bringing back on her the Austrian dukes, a Papal sovereign, and the Bourbon of Naples. The English *Tories* were then greatly to blame, for they might have saved much. But in 1848 our Whigs were as bad, both in regard to Sicily and the Austrian dukes; and now, when Rome fell under the attack of

Louis Napoleon, and some miserable Romans fled with women and children in crazy ill-found vessels to Malta, the governor forbade their landing. They were forced to continue dangerous navigation, not knowing to what port of safety! Joseph Hume asked in Parliament of our Foreign Secretary (Lord John Russell), whether the Governor of Malta had received orders to repel the fugitives, and received the bitter reply, that "there had been no time to give orders, but the governor's conduct was entirely approved; for these fugitives had made (?) a revolution in Rome, and no doubt would do the same in Malta *if they could.*" I am forced to quote the words by mere memory; but they went deep into many English hearts beside mine, as showing how demoralizing is the atmosphere of an English Cabinet. (In the American civil war, Earl Russell displayed a like hatred of Americans for their Republicanism. No wonder that he favoured Austrians in the Italian movement against Austria, and afterwards threatened Italy with the English fleet, if Garibaldi or

Cavour interfered with "*English interests*" in the Adriatic, whatever these may have meant.)

Digression on Lord John Russell.

In 1860 Lord John's utterance elicited from me the following paper:—

What has Lord John confessed?

1. He used the name of England to hinder Kossuth from being director of an Italian railway. 2. He tries to keep Austria up.

I remark on this—

I. Austria is not a "Conservative" Power, but a "Revolutionist." It is mere Radical Revolution, which wants to cut away the present from the past, and that is what Austria wants.

Her conduct (1) in Spain, (2) in Holland, (3) in Bohemia, (4) in Vienna, (5) in Hungary, (6) in Venetia and Milan, all prove it.

What right has England to claim that Hungary will trust this dynasty?

II. This present emperor is illegal.

He is a usurper, put on the throne by Russian arms.

Remember the treachery to the patriot generals hanged at Arad.

Remember Louis Batthyanyi, ambassador of peace.

Remember this man's *Concordat* with the pope, and his *plundering of funds* destined to religion and to education.

Remember the *National bankruptcies* of Austria.

III. What chance has the English Government of succeeding?

Hungary remembers she has conquered Austria.

Russia will not help again.

Servia and Croatia will not be cheated again.

The Tyrol and Bohemia are discontented.

The Stadion Constitution is exploded.

Italy and Garibaldi are come into existence!

The English Stock Exchange is sick of Austria; so is that of Vienna.

Napoleon also is sick of the Pope.

IV. What is the cure? The *disease* is, the meddling of the English ministry to help despotism.

But Napoleon believed that the pope's ingratitude to him was inspired by trust in Austria. When the Crimean war ended (1856), not without brave aid from Sardinian and Piedmontese troops, the allies had no cause to thank Austria; and Count Cavour (Sardinian minister) spoke up bravely for Italy in the Congress. Louis Napoleon honoured his own uncle's policy to Italy, probably disliked a Bourbon dynasty in Naples, and felt keenly the hatred and danger which his restoration of the pope had earned; as well as humiliation from inability to fulfil his promise to England. The obstinate Pio IX. reigned in Rome solely by support of the French garrison, yet believed he might insult his patron, and defy him. Already, in 1856, Napoleon and Cavour had come closer together, and before long Cavour saw that Kossuth was an ally not to be thrown away.

Moreover, that staunch Napoleonist, Persigny (for I afterwards learnt it was he), had enticed Kossuth into a continuous correspondence. Kossuth explained to me why he allowed it. He had found that Persigny read all Kossuth's letters to the emperor, and reported the comments made on them. Kossuth valued the opportunity of setting the emperor right as to facts, perhaps of refuting Austrian slanders, and in one way or other hoped for good to his country from this strange correspondence. From another quarter I heard, and I easily believed, that the emperor, knowing how sharply the want of political funds must cripple Kossuth, ordered Persigny to ply him with hints, that if in any matter they could profitably act in concert, money should not be any difficulty. Kossuth, in leaving Hungary, had not even asked for his wages as Governor, lest slander should stick to him. Some one further told me (whether truly I cannot say) that Kossuth's sharpest insults against Napoleon were uttered to secure himself against yielding to pecuniary temptation, if hard pressed, and so losing his uprightness. He did not then know how thick of skin was this notable emperor.

More than one Italian attempt at the life of Napoleon was reported, and in the end of 1857 (?) came the really formidable attack by Count Orsini, a patriotic Italian, who no doubt held the old Greek doctrine of Timoleon, Brutus, and Cicero, which proved deadly to Caius Julius. A copy of the passage of Seneca de Irâ, in which he recounts how Augustus ended attempts to assassinate him *by forgiving* (at his wife's advice) the last who made it, was sent by post anonymously to the French emperor. Presently a Hungarian exile in Paris (a regular correspondent, I believe) reported to my friends as a certainty that Napoleon *would have* forgiven Orsini, only that several faithful Frenchmen had been killed by Orsini's terrible explosive; therefore Napoleon dared not forgive, but spoke kindly and confidentially to him. Orsini went to his death calmly, and from the scaffold exhorted all Italians to trust to the generous intentions of the emperor.

The increasing intimacy of Napoleon with Cavour was eagerly watched by my Hungarian friends, who augured that if France aided Italy, *that* must weaken Austria, and ere long aid Hungary. Napoleon was striving to attain for his dynasty the stability of a constitutional throne, and issued edicts to increase freedom of speech in the legislative assembly. The immediate result was that Republican members frightened him by attacking his dynasty, or at least so he interpreted their sallies. A missive from Cavour once followed, to this effect, "No more hope for us this year. The emperor is so frightened by the Republicans, that he throws himself on to the clergy, and will do nothing that will displease them." This tiding drew out from Kossuth a characteristic utterance. "Ah!" said he, "these French Republicans mean well; but, through hatred to Napoleon, they fail to see this right course. He dares not contend against them and the clergy both together. If they would relax their enmity to him, so far as to *aid him* to weaken the Church and make himself independent of it, they would soon find that he would be forced to court them and make large concessions. But while they think of Napoleon as their mortal enemy, they forget that the Church is their immortal enemy."

The next foreign event to which I need to allude is the marriage announced to impend— I think late in 1858—between Prince Napoleon and Princess Clotilde, daughter of the King of Sardinia. Kossuth was at once excited at the news, and said to me, "I have always resisted Napoleon's overtures, but I expect now that I shall be forced to visit him in Paris." "Why so?" said I, in astonishment. "Because I now see," said he, "that he is resolved upon war against Austria. This Piedmontese marriage is evidently his pledge of alliance with Sardinia; his pledge also to Italians that he means to drive Austria out of Italy." I too *then* believed that Orsini's dying words meant something. No English newspaper, as far as I know, was half so clearsighted; but Kossuth at once perceived that if Napoleon made war on Austria, he could not forget that Austria was assailable in Croatia. Moreover, the Austrian Cabinet, with blind infatuation, no sooner had crushed Hungary, than it made itself hated by the Croatians and Bohemians, whom it had stirred up against Hungary by invectives on "the proud Magyars;" but after their fall, the other populations found that they were *all* crushed down into a *common* and worse slavery. New hope quickly arose in Kossuth, *if* Napoleon were bent on war.

When the new year (1859) dawned, a few calm words, moderate in sound, yet most unexpectedly unfriendly to Austria, were addressed to her ambassador by the French emperor, and threw panic into every European *bourse*. The season of the year forbade military action, but war was felt to be intended, and Russia was no longer a support to Austria behind. Not to be tedious, before the spring opened the Alps, Kossuth and Pulszky were actually invited to Paris, and were received at the station most cordially by Prince Napoleon, cousin to the emperor. The details were minutely communicated to me by Pulszky, and the outline remains fixed in my memory.

In order, if possible, to set them both quite at ease, the prince opened abruptly, after his first words of welcome, as follows :—" You know, gentlemen, that a little while ago we were enemies. Well, that was inevitable, because at that time our interests were opposed. But now circumstances are greatly changed. We should blame ourselves greatly, if, from any resentment perpetuated from the time when events made us enemies, we should damage ourselves by refusal to co-operate with you, when our interests, if not identical, yet run parallel. You do not aim at the very same objects as we do, but you may promote your own objects by helping in some way, and thus serve yourselves by dropping any resentment for the past. And let me assure you, this is precisely the temperament of the emperor. He is a man without loves and without hatreds. He studies only for the immediate object to be won, and never indulges a resentment that would damage him. Not but that I would venture to suggest to M. Kossuth, that on consideration he might find it expedient to withdraw any superfluous phrases which here and there he has launched against the emperor."

Here Kossuth interposed, and said, "If the emperor will do something to secure treaty-rights and justice for my country, he will secure from me high panegyric and warm thanks, in full proportion to all my assaults on him."

The prince appeared to receive this promise graciously, and the interview continued quite harmoniously. When, after this, they were introduced to the emperor himself, his frankness and simplicity forbade any dread of insincerity; for he never professed to have any desire to help Hungary, only in certain contingencies to help himself through the Hungarians. They were equally frank; thus their colloquies were harmonious and satisfactory. As they may previously have augured, his main desire was, in case his war against Austria could not be concluded in Italy itself, and he needed to send an army into Croatia, to get counsel from Kossuth as to numerous details; such as, on what islands off the coast will it be expedient to land? What landing places shall I select with a view to marching to Agram? On what provisions for an army may I count? What is the state and length of military roads? Kossuth undertook, under certain conditions, to furnish in prescribed time full naval and military information. I believe he acquitted himself of the task at no distant day; but before the French troops could enter Italy a new alarm from England distressed Napoleon seriously. The late Lord Derby was our Tory Premier, who wished well to Austria.

Some retrospect of the previous three years in England is now needful.

After the conclusion of peace with Russia, Lord Palmerston was very grand. The Aberdeenites had been discredited; so had Lord John Russell; Palmerston perhaps counted himself a great hero. He had risen at first as a follower of Mr. Canning, who was an essentially Liberal Tory, and he had passed over to Lord Grey as a Whig. Ever since 1832 he had been the inevitable Foreign Minister of the Whigs, until he mortally offended the Prince Consort (as we must now infer) by his desire to shield his despatches from the sight of Baron Stockmâr. A Viennese newspaper (shown to me) had announced his impending ejection by the influence of "an illustrious person in England," in order to bring the Cabinets of Schonbrün and St. James's into closer agreement. The date of the paper was earlier than Palmerston's ejection was known in London. But Lord John Russell, though unable to defend Palmerston from royal attack, no doubt sided with him. He was soon back in office, but this time as Home Secretary, and quickly established himself in work as a diligent man, resolved to know everything for himself, and to be lord, not slave, of the unchanging officers. His vigour in this new position raised him high in esteem. Yet he did not intermit his old arts. "Pam," with a straw in his mouth, still figured in the sporting magazines, and he was believed still to keep several "organs" of news in his special interest. Despite of royal dislike, he had risen to be the foremost man in England. He professed to lead the Liberals, yet had too much of the Tory to encounter Tory antagonism. Was it wonderful if he became somewhat elated? His sobriety was not equal to his fortune. He was certainly too full of grand projects. The late Sir John Bowring, in defence of his bombardment of Canton (March, 1857), said to me in the hearing of a large company, "When the despatches sent to me from home are all published, it will be seen that I had no choice but to do what I did." Our Parliament was shocked at the cruel, and every way unjustifiable, bombardment. Some who computed dates closely, asserted that the gunboats which had been built too late for the Crimean war, were sent out to Sir John Bowring before any news had arrived of the imprisonment of the Chinese pirate who had bought the use of the English flag. To punish this imprisonment, the innocent people of Canton had been bombarded! Parliament passed a vote of censure on Sir John Bowring, and Palmerston punished the vote by a penal dissolution! While he was preparing a war against China, the Indian Mutiny burst upon us. In the new Parliament his arrogance gave more and more offence; indeed, the flames of Pekin which he kindled may yet, as the Marquis Tseng sufficiently indicates, entrain retribution on England. A sudden movement against Palmerston had a success which no one can have anticipated. Nothing short of deep disgust in his own party can explain it.

Napoleon, after Orsini's dangerous attack, was naturally sensitive and anxious as to the facilities of plotting assassination in London which English freedom allowed. On his complaint, Palmerston, as an earnest friend, rashly made too off-hand a promise of redress, and proceeded, as if to tamper with our freedom was not a very delicate task. This suddenly brought upon him, from a very mild and peace-loving man, Milner Gibson, a friend of Cobden, the grave accusation of dishonouring England by wrongful concessions to foreign demand of change in our laws. The attack was supported by so much zeal (which, I confess, to me seemed like malicious bitterness) that Palmerston resigned office. I conclude that he discerned how fatally he had lost the hearts of many of his supporters, and that prolonged office would be uneasy and inglorious. This move brought in a Tory ministry, with the late Lord Derby as Premier.

When, in 1859, a Franco-Austrian war impended, and the preparations in France more and more portended a reality, the strong bias of the Tory policy towards Austria was variously indicated and made Napoleon very uneasy. The English Liberals were now perhaps already repenting that they had discarded Palmerston, whose "Hungarian speech" had shown great contempt of Austrian alliance, while Austria had been the desire of Aberdeen, of Clarendon, and of Lord John Russell; and now a fear arose lest, though Austria had refused to aid *us*, yet Lord Derby might suddenly aid *her*. Sympathy with injured Italy was felt by many who had been hard-hearted to Hungary, and the anxiety fermented in all lovers of freedom. Kossuth detailed to me Napoleon's secret talk with him. It ran thus—

"You have influence with many in England. If you are able, your best service for me at present will be, to drive this Lord Derby out of office. I frankly tell you my position. The French army is very formidable; but I cannot pretend that in it I have such superiority to Austria, that I may expect easy or certain success. My only clear superiority is on the sea. As Louis Philippe before me, so have I from the first carefully nursed my fleet. Hereby I override Austria in the Adriatic—a most critical advantage. Now, this Lord Derby brings to me first one and then another demand which clearly shows his enmity, and alarms me as to what he may do. *I cannot forget Copenhagen nor Navarino.* I cannot be sure but that, without declaring war or giving warning, he may all at once strike a blow which will annihilate my fleet: and then what could compensate me? If you can find any way of moving discontent against this ministry, I want you to cripple or eject him."

Kossuth did not tell me his reply. I was chiefly struck by the frank confession how great was Napoleon's terror at our fleet, which convinced me that our panic about his imputed scheme of invasion in 1853 was an entire though natural mistake. I make no doubt that Kossuth set before the emperor that it would be worse than futile for *him* as a foreigner to take any side publicly in English party-quarrels; only through Liberal friends the exiles might privately urge the monstrosity of injuring Italy for the sake of Austrian archdukes. Presently, I think, both he and Pulszky visited Cavour in Turin, where, as afterwards appeared, the representative of England (Sir James Hudson) set secret detectives to dog every step that Kossuth took!

Gradually the party of *freedom* in England, was turned more and more into a *peace* party, from dread of Lord Derby's bias to Austria. The will and resolve to eject him was gathering strength, but the Parliamentary opposition took up quite other grounds. D'Israeli was for the second time Chancellor of the Exchequer. He and his chief believed (for reasons which need no mention here) that some extension of the suffrage was inevitable, and wished to have the credit of carrying it, while making it as little democratic as possible. D'Israeli's "fancy-franchises" were *laughed down* and defeated roughly at the end of March. A new Parliament was convened, still less manageable, and Lord Derby resigned in June. He was followed by Palmerston as Premier, and Napoleon at last breathed freely.

The weather had delayed the passing of the Alps by the French army, yet on May 20 the allies defeated the Austrians at Montebello. On June 4 followed a great and decisive battle at Magenta. Pulszky must have returned to England, for I remember going to him and asking, "Did you see, that, according to the

Times, when Napoleon was anxiously waiting for MacMahon's arrival, which gave him the victory, MacMahon was able to effect the junction only by two Hungarian regiments coming over to him?" "Yes, I saw it," Pulszky eagerly replied, "and we have written to Cavour to learn whether it is true." On a later day he told me, that, in exact truth, not two Hungarian regiments, but one Hungarian and one Croatian regiment, came over. The Hungarians laid down their arms to MacMahon, but the Croatians first killed their (Austrian) officers.

The importance of this was extreme. It showed that the strength of the Austrian army was not proportionate to its numbers, and they were now likely to be embarrassed by distrust of their own troops. This also seemed to explain their sudden evacuation of Placenza, and dismantling of its forts, when no enemy was near. The people of Milan, indeed, rose after the battle of Magenta, and drove out the Austrian garrison. Danger may justly have been feared by the Austrian commanders from many quarters.

Their armies had to retreat beyond the river Mincio, concentrating their forces; and the Emperor Francis Joseph came in person to take the command. The Franco-Sardinians, in united strength, soon struck the final blow, on June 24, on the battlefield of Solferino. Along the heights of Volta the Austrians had formidable batteries, which swept the smooth slopes up which the adverse forces had to march. Kossuth afterwards told me, that through curiosity he later walked over the field, and it at once was clear to him, that if Russian or English cannoniers had had to work the batteries, no army in the world could have marched up without losing all cohesive power. Yet in this battle the estimated loss of the Austrians was far greater than that of the allies. Evidently the Croatian cannoniers must have *purposely* fired over the heads of the enemy. So too did the Austrians judge, according to the report of the *Times*' commissioner (Mr.

Gallenga?) soon after the battle, where victory, it seems, was irrecoverable when the batteries were passed. This commissioner, writing, I think, from Mantua, notified the fierce resentment of Austrian officers at the mere sight of any Croatian soldier. At such a one they would at once make a cut with whip or cane, scolding him as one of the traitors who had ruined their cause at Solferino. This second perfidy of their own troops seems to have shaken all confidence out of the Austrians. Kossuth was convinced, he told me, that if Napoleon had summoned Mantua to surrender, the Austrians would not have dared to fight again, so deep was the dismay and distrust. His hopes rose high, that the allies would conquer all Venetia in a rush, and be soon ready to cross the Adriatic. But he was suddenly struck with deep disappointment by tidings of the peace of Villafranca, concluded between Francis Joseph of Austria and Louis Napoleon.

Napoleon had proclaimed to all Italy freedom

from the Austrian yoke; now he made peace without liberating Venetia. Plenty of English writers jibed against him, and for many months our newspapers seemed deaf or incredulous to the plain frank statements made by Napoleon to the legislature of Paris—though it was corroborated by the boast of the King of Prussia to the Parliament of Berlin, that he had arrested the war by threatening to join his forces with those of Austria, if French troops crossed the Adriatic. Napoleon to the Parisian legislature said, that, on receiving this announcement from Berlin, he found that to persevere in hostility would bring France into a double war—one with Austria in the South, a second with Prussia on the Rhine. Victory in such a contest would demand immense sacrifice from France, and with no commensurate reward to her. He could not bear to ask it, but must be contented with having won for Italy a large fraction of what he desired, though not everything. (I write from memory, and cannot give his very words.)

Kossuth knew nothing as yet of the intervention of Prussia, and stayed at Turin in much gloom, yet studied his own claims, while forced to admit that in nothing had Napoleon been unfaithful. A French minister came to him at Turin, with official notice of the peace of Villafranca, and a direct question from Napoleon, whether Kossuth had any demands on him. All had been duly preconsidered, so that in a few minutes the clear reply came out, "Sir, I have two demands on your master: *First*, he must extract from the Emperor Francis Joseph an amnesty for every Hungarian or Croatian soldier who has taken military service under the King of Sardinia. *Secondly*, no man thus amnestied shall ever be pressed into the Austrian army." The French minister commented on this, "Sir, I have little doubt that your first request will be obtained; but I beg you to drop your second request, for I fear it is simply impossible." "Upon this," said Kossuth to me, "I stiffened myself up into as much pride as I could put on, and replied sharply, 'Forgive me, sir, if I mistake; but did you not tell me that your master commanded you to ask me whether I had any demands on him, and if any, then what they were?'" "Certainly," said the French minister; "such were my words." "Good," said Kossuth. "My demands on your master are the two which I have now set before you; and I entirely decline any discussion with you about them." So the French minister took his leave. 'It would have been useless," said Kossuth to me, "to obtain the first point without the second; for if the men were once ranged in the Austrian army, amnesty would not avail them from endless hardship and torment through cruel spite. The certainty of this forced me to insist on my second demand."

A fortnight elapsed before Kossuth heard the result: Francis Joseph had given way on both points. The Hungarians, from the slowness of concession, inferred that Napoleon had found the extortion of it no easy task. To complete this affair, I skip on for a year perhaps. Reports had reached Pulszky and Kossuth in London that certain Hungarians thus amnestied had been forced into the Austrian army. The two got definite, formal, and authenticated evidence of each fact from Hungary, and sent all the documents to Paris for Napoleon. In due time they learnt that they had been sent to the French ambassador at Vienna, with orders to lay the case before the Emperor Francis Joseph, with solemn comments, which *were interpreted* to threaten renewal of war; perhaps only smoothly saying that Napoleon looked on the deeds as an infraction of the peace of Villafranca. Anyhow, he so pressed the matter home to Francis Joseph that all the men were discharged from the service. That Baron Beust, the Saxon minister, had already whispered counsel into Francis Joseph's ear is not probable; but the Austrian emperor may already have discerned in his military disasters, that his only safe course was to reconcile himself to Hungary.

I go back to the peace of Villafranca in its results on England. A most absurd report spread far and wide (afterwards imputed—perhaps quite falsely—to Orleanite craft) that Austria and France had laid down their quarrel, in order to attack England by a joint invasion, while she was unprepared, and *therefore* we immediately needed a great VOLUNTEER ARMY. The silly report was in Palmerston's interest, and, by the rule of the Roman Cassius ("Cui bono?" *i.e.* WHÓ GAINS BY IT?), was manufactured in Palmerstonian circles. Palmerston always desired a large militia, as a feeder to the standing army, and now he wanted an army of volunteers for home defence, that he might be free to send abroad to India, South Africa, or other parts a larger fraction of the regular army. In 1857-8 was the formidable Indian Mutiny, and the native troops being less trustworthy, an increase of our British army there was judged inevitable. But besides, he made war against Persia, against Canton, and against Pekin itself, and all Asia seemed to need armies from England. I cannot assert, but I heard and believed, that Palmerston promoted the volunteer movement to the utmost of his power. Many Radicals, though lovers of peace, joined the volunteers, *partly* from a sense that our national defence ought to be in a trained and *inoffensive* populace, not in an OFFENSIVE NAVY; *partly* from a self-contempt at their own ignorance how to use a rifle. But the volunteers, becoming half paid and directed by the central executive, are not local and free, like the trained bands of our old cities.

My Hungarian friends, by reason of their profound interest in Italy, quitted England in 1860, after Garibaldi's wonderful exploits, and these pages naturally end at their departure. But some of Kossuth's last words to me will be of interest to the English public. "Louis Napoleon," said he, "is a man at whom, on account of his *coup d'état*, I shudder; and it may seem a duty to hate him. Yet I am bound to say, not only has he been wholly faithful to us, but every time I have been closeted with him. I have come away with a higher opinion, not only of his talents and sagacity, but also of his morals."

Kossuth's two sons became civil engineers in Italy; so, naturally, he remains there. Finding himself unable to direct and restrain those in Hungary who called themselves Kossuth's party, he at last formally withdrew from all politics. Thenceforward he is visited by Hungarians of every colour; and, Pulszky informs me, he is by all regarded as a most agreeable and estimable old gentleman. His birth-year was 1801.

Pulszky was readmitted to Hungary when Francis Joseph, after learning wisdom by his Italian disasters, desired to make his Reichsrath a parliament like that of England. Foiled by the rivalries of his different kingdoms, and pushed out of Germany by the Prussian Seven Days' war, he called Baron Beust, a celebrated Saxon statesman, to his aid, and by his sage advice established himself as a thoroughly constitutional monarch. Pulszky became his Finance Minister, and received his public thanks for reconciling the interests of Hungary and Austria. The monarchy is at length called

Dual, because Hungary, with its provincial appanages balances Bohemia, Austria, and her provinces, with Gallicia or the Polish remnant. In fact, it appears that *Kossuth's demand is now practically satisfied.* All the empire has constitutions of local freedom, and Hungary, as the most powerful member, stands forth like an eldest son. Amnesty has been blessedly complete on both sides. The emperor was legitimately crowned King of Hungary in 1867, with all Hungarian historical legality. He has been faithful, and the Hungarians thoroughly recognize it. The change in eighteen years was happy and marvellous. Pulszky, born in 1814, has returned to his old beloved studies, and lives in the Museum at Buda-Pest.

PRINTED BY WILLIAM CLOWES AND SONS, LIMITED,
LONDON AND BECCLES.

www.ingramcontent.com/pod-product-compliance
Lightning Source LLC
Chambersburg PA
CBHW022134160426
43197CB00009B/1279